Seeing to Understand:

YOUR SCIENTIFIC THINKING LIFESTYLE COACH

Panos Efsta

Healthcare ebook: 978-1-7339059-2-3
Healthcare Spiral Bound book: 978-1-7339059-0-9
Healthcare Perfect Bound book: 978-1-7339059-4-7
Library of Congress Control Number 2019908692

Cover art created by Panos & Kate Efsta
Design by Panos & Kate Efsta
Illustrations by Panos Efsta

Printed in the United States of America.

Second edition 2019.

Global Lean Enterprises LLC
pe@piellc.us

www.piellc.us

FOR PRACTITIONERS IN THE HEALTHCARE (HOSPITALS & MEDICAL CLINICS) INDUSTRY

What makes this book different?

Seeing to Understand is your scientific thinking lifestyle coach. This coach will help you turn your daily thinking into an intentional process instead of a random practice. After reading it, you will better understand and practice the scientific thinking lifestyle. It evolves your thinking's DNA structure by synthesizing Data Analysis, Training Within Industry, and KATA in a simplified, yet breakthrough manner. This coach accompanies you everywhere. You help evolve it with your reflections and make it your own. No two coaches are going to be alike. Scientific thinking is not a project or something we apply at certain times or only at work. It is a lifestyle. It is designed to help you have fun applying it everywhere. Regardless of your profession, title, organization, or education, this coach will guide you in your quest to understand and practice the scientific thinking lifestyle. Join me in this innovative and inquisitive journey full of discoveries and exploration where nothing you experience is arbitrary or unintentional.

Dedication

My wife and I dedicate this coach to all the doctors, nurses, medical, and administrative staff around the globe who work tirelessly every day to save lives. To my brother, Taso; your life and wisdom as a healer impacted everyone you touched. You are sorely missed! And to my new friend, Hogan, who at just three years old, bravely and resolutely stands strong in his fight to overcome leukemia. May your spirit and energy be a beacon of light shining the way for all who suffer! And, to the many caregivers around the world, I owe you my sincerest thanks for your ardent dedication to saving lives. Because of you, I am living my dream of being a scientific lifestyle coach dedicated to enhancing and healing lives!

Acknowledgments

I WOULD LIKE TO give thanks and honor to God for granting me the wisdom and understanding to write this coach at lightning speed. His strength gave me the fortitude and insight I needed to share my gifts with the world. I thank you, Lord!

I would also like to thank my God-sent wife. Her support was instrumental for me to put together this coach. She is my most ardent cheerleader, and without her masterful editing assistance, I could not have put together all my thoughts and experiences with love and passion, for all the amazing people around the globe who enjoy learning. I love you, baby doll!

I can never forget one of my favorite mentors, Tom Robers, whose passion and belief in my ability to think critically and innovatively gave me the confidence to step out on faith.

I would also like to thank Brandon Brown, Skip Steward, and Patrick Graupp for sharing their knowledge, which influenced me to evolve my thinking and developing this coach.

I could not have developed this coach without the inspiration and lessons I learned in the healthcare field, from the medical staff at Baptist Memorial Health Care and Bryan Health. You are an incredible group of caregivers and gave me more than I could ever offer you!

I would also like to highlight the excellent work of the Jack Welch Management Institute MBA professors, particularly, Jason Gateas, John Bennett and Kirstin Leighton-Lucas.

Finally, I would like to thank everyone who helped me review and edit this coach, including Professor Sylvain Landry, Tracy Defoe, Maurene Stock, and many others. Thank you for helping me simplify concepts, correct errors, and make it practical for those who work on improving their work daily. I am grateful to all of you.

Special Thanks to:

Sara Hennessy

Lyndsey Mart

Jill Geschke

Keri Cartagena

Susan Brown

Linda Stones

Samantha Penas

Tracy Loveless

Kimberly Anderson

Mindy Greenrod

Becca Berner

Parker Harris

Madalyn Mason

Kimberly Allen

Melinda Wolfe

Cara Beard

Pallis Wilson

Karen Clark

Judy Mann

Tabetha Polly

Jan Padgett

Julie Bennet

Zachary Brent

Elizabeth Mills

Dawn Waddell

Kati Boswell

Jana Crittenden

Lee Ann Ross

James Grantham

Kathy Bennett

Carol Bubnick

Jeannie Walker

Chad Sanders

Lindsey Brady

Sherrita Lovelace

Dan Nitz

Dave List

Adrienne Bryant

Maxwell Schwam

Robert Williard

Heather Greenland

Toya Dabney

Melanie Mays

Michelle Peck

Ashley Dufrene

Sandy Boyle

Tim Bradshaw

Vicki Harden-Balash

Lily Fettes

Kati Boswell

Donald J. Wheeler

Chip & Dan Heath

PLEASE REFER TO THIS BOOK AS YOUR
SCIENTIFIC THINKING LIFESTYLE COACH.

AFTER YOU FINISH READING
EACH CHAPTER, ASK YOURSELF:
"WHAT HAVE I LEARNED?"

ALWAYS DOCUMENT YOUR REFLECTIONS
AS THEY WILL HELP YOU IDENTIFY
AND PURSUE YOUR PURPOSE

What People Are Saying

In Seeing to Understand, Panos Efsta is calling you to take a step of action. He is encouraging you to take a step to be less dependent on consultants. He is cheering you to take a step to create skills versus just gaining more knowledge. He is inspiring us to be intentional and take a STEP forward.
—*Skip Steward, Vice President and Chief Improvement Officer, Baptist Memorial Health Care*

This book is a detailed practice guide to improvement using scientific thinking. Panos' enthusiasm for learning is contagious!
—*Maurene Stock, Senior Performance Excellence Consultant, Mercy Health*

This book is a must-read for everyone who wants to begin or is currently practicing KATA or other improvement methodology. Whether it's your first time reading through it or your 100th time referencing it, you will learn something new or deepen your understanding of the concepts within. Now that I know what lies within, I won't practice KATA without it within reach. I feel so much more confident in my competency on the concepts presented after reading this book. I now feel that I know the concepts well enough to follow the guide and lean on the process to show the way when I feel unsure of a way forward. With our team and your words, our potential is limitless.
—*Sara Hennessy, Nursing Manager, Bryan Health*

Scientific problem solving is a learned practice that does not come natural to us. Human nature tends to lead by assumptions, jump to solutions before understanding, and fight fires instead of identifying and addressing root causes. Seeing to Understand is a great resource to practice scientific problem solving. As "repetition is the mother of all learning" no one can learn a new skill-- let alone a new way of thinking--without regular daily practice. Learning to See serves as a daily life coach to practice scientific problem solving thinking. The appendix at the end on Process Behavior Charts was very helpful in trying to understand that tool and its application!

—Tom Frederick, Continuous Improvement Practitioner, Michigan Medicine

Seeing To Understand is a think outside the box way to reach goals. Eliminating the obstacles in the way of the result you want to achieve, places an entirely new perspective on goal setting. It allows you to seek the true reason you cannot reach goals and makes one think in an unbiased manner about their true knowledge of a situation. You will reach goals you never thought possible!!

—Jana Crittenden, Chief Nursing Officer, Baptist Memorial Health Care

Enseigner efficacement la pensée scientifique (Toyota Kata). Apprendre à décomposer le travail, à revoir le processus et à enseigner la nouvelle méthode tout en renforçant la relation avec les individus (TWI). Favoriser l'utilisation d'outils statistiques simples et efficaces (chartes de comportement des processus) pour percevoir les signaux à travers le bruit (ou variation naturelle) et confirmer l'impact ou non des changements sur la performance du processus. Panos Efsta à su rassembler et intégrer le résultat de ses apprentissages dans un ouvrage de référence axé sur la pratique, étape par étape. Que vous débutiez ou que vous ayez déjà beaucoup pratiqué, vous retrouverez dans « Seeing to understand », plusieurs astuces et pièges à évitez qui vous amènerons à réfléchir sur la manière dont vous développez le potentiel de vos équipes. Mon Apprenti est mon «Storyboard». Merci Panos!

Teach effectively scientific thinking (Toyota Kata). Learn to break down the work, review the process and teach the new method while strengthening the relationship with individuals (TWI). Promote the use of simple and effective statistical tools (PBC) to perceive the signals through the noise (or natural variation) and confirm the impact or not of the changes on the performance of the process. Panos Efsta has been able to gather and integrate the results of its learning in a reference book focused on practice, step by step. Whether you are starting out or have already practiced a lot, you will find in "Seeing to understand" several tips and pitfalls to avoid which will lead you to think about how you develop the potential of your teams. My Apprentice is my Storyboard. Thank you Panos!
—*Philippe Deslandes, Performance Advisor at CSSS Haut-Richelieu – Rouville*

Great resource for learning to think differently and approach problems from an adaptive problem-solving mindset.
—*Anonymous*

Seeing to Understand is an essential resource for all that have begun or are continuing their process improvement journey. This 'how to' guide connects the dots between data analysis, KATA and Training Within Industry in a straight forward manner that truly helps your team understand and move forward with the concepts. It is packed with excellent examples as well as thought-provoking Reflection Points. I highly recommend it.

—*Karen Clark, Point of Care Supervisor, Baptist Memorial Health Care*

Definitions

CC: Current Condition represents all the details related to the current state of a focus process.

JI: Job Instruction is a four-step process designed to develop the capability of an employee on a specific job through training and validation, to create stability in the process (a form of standard work).

JM: Job Methods is a four-step process that leads one to understand the current state of a process and through a defined set of six questions develop a proposed state (a form of a Kaizen event).

JR: Job Relations is a four-step process that guides on to resolve a conflict, as well as invest on its four foundations to help proactively build good relations.

KATA: Improvement and coaching KATA is the foundation of scientific thinking necessary to guide us through the steps of process improvement by expanding our threshold of knowledge through continuous obstacle-hunting and experimentation.

Learner: Anyone, regardless of their title, who wishes to develop her/his skill and learning through rigorous obstacle hunting and enjoy improving the work.

LNPL: Lower Natural Process Limit is a horizontal line below the mean, depicting a calculated limit as part of the process behavior charts.

mR: Moving Range showcases the variation between two consecutive values.

PDSA: Plan Do Study Act

SIPOC: Suppliers, Inputs, Process, Outputs, and Customer are a source of information that helps create a high-level overview process map.

TC: Target Condition represents all the details related to the focus process at future (typically two-weeks out) state.

TWI: Training Within Industry is a dynamic program that helps teach the necessary skills for employees to deal with process improvements, job training, job safety, as well as managing conflict effectively and creating a good relations environment.

UNPL: Upper Natural Process Limit is a horizontal line above the mean, depicting a calculated limit as part of the process behavior charts.

VOC: Voice of the Customer describes a customer's feedback about the expectations for the product or service they are willing to pay.

VOP: Voice of the Process describes the visual representation of the process data, in such a way that allows us to understand what the process it trying to tell us.

X-Bar: The line depicted on a run chart representing the mean (average) of a dataset.

XmR: The line depicted on a run chart representing the mean (average) of the dataset's moving range.

1st Coach: Anyone, regardless of their title, who constantly coaches the learner to find and pursue her/his purpose of improving the work and enjoys developing capability through the good coaching foundations.

2nd Coach: Anyone, regardless of their title, who frequently coaches the 1st coach to find and pursue her/his purpose of developing the capability of the learner.

Contents

AS YOU JOURNEY THROUGH LIFE, YOU
WILL ENCOUNTER MANY CHALLENGES.

TAKE THE TIME TO SAVOR THE
SWEET MOMENTS AND CHERISH
THE WISDOM YOU HAVE EARNED.

The Moral of the Story

IMAGINE THE FOLLOWING SCENARIO: You walk into your local hospital's emergency room complaining of abdominal pain on your right side. The nursing staff sees you are in significant pain and asks what your pain level is on a scale of 1 to 10. You respond in agony that your pain level is 15. The staff immediately calls the doctor in, and upon meeting with you, states he is preparing you for surgery. He says this without taking any tests, drawing any blood, or undertaking any other assessment. He then tells you everything is going to be just fine. If you were the patient in this scenario, how would you feel?

Now, put yourself in the doctor's position and reflect on a process you have improved upon in the past. Think about how you would have addressed the above scenario. Did you conduct a patient analysis and experiment with different approaches? Or did you, like the doctor, leap into problem-solving mode without examining other options?

This coach will help you learn how to approach your continuous improvement processes using the scientific thinking method.

Identify Your Storyboard

Figure 1: Identify & look only at your storyboard; not its reflection

IT IS THE CONTEXT behind our thinking, actions, and even data that matters. You are not going to do this alone. The effectiveness of the relationship among the improvement team members is foundational in the achievement of any performance challenge. The pawn below is your learner. He is working on his storyboard challenge. His challenge is to find out how to become king. As his coach, how would you advise your pawn? Would you focus on helping him become king, or try to influence his thinking so that he grasps the process of becoming a king on his own? Which choice is sustainable?

In the above scenario, the pawn is a learner you can have a direct impact upon. The reflection of the learner is the storyboard. The only way you can impact the storyboard (reflection) is by influencing the learner (pawn). Regardless of what you do to the wall, the reflection will remain the same. Your job is to work with your learner, influence her thinking, and help create the "reflection" of a winner. Performance graphs on the walls will not change anything unless we work on improving the performance of each process. It does not matter how many improvement storyboards we have or how disciplined our teams are but how quickly we develop capability among our employees and influence them towards the scientific thinking lifestyle. Neither will lead to a winning team who believes and acts on the main purpose: Improving the work is the work, and it is fun. Do we want our employees to come to work each day just to accomplish their daily tasks? Or do we want them to come in, begin hunting for obstacles, experiment, learn, and constantly grown their competency that leads to the innovation of the process' performance?

Throughout my career, I have experienced improvement teams that said: "We have to KATA at 2 pm", or "When do you want to Kata with us?" I responded by asking them to replace the word "KATA" with "THINK" and repeat the sentence: "We have to THINK at 2 pm,", or "When do you want to THINK with us?" This change must have impacted my team because we began thinking in new and different ways.

This coach will help you turn your daily thinking into an intentional process instead of a random practice. After reading it, you will better understand and practice the scientific thinking lifestyle. It evolves your thinking's DNA structure by synthesizing Data Analysis, TWI, and KATA in a simplified manner.

Storyboard

A STORYBOARD IS NOT just a whiteboard full of data and charts. It takes different forms, and its elements truly matter. If we do not understand the context, we will operate in a surreal rather than real environment, improving imaginary conditions, and celebrating assumptions on our data analysis.

You may be partnering with this coach because you are struggling in your continuous improvement initiatives. You have difficulty identifying, from the available data, how impactful your improvements have been. Executives push solutions and try to get known best practices in-house, but on some level, they do not understand and support you to overcome the obstacles you are facing. Why is our performance better on some days than others? What does it mean when that is the case? Is our current improvement system working for us? Does it help develop the skill and competency among our employees? Probably not as we had hoped.

I apologize in advance for what I am about to say here, but, you do not know, and therefore, cannot understand your current condition. You have been operating under a solution-based model which has resulted in organizational chaos. Do not fret; we have been a victim of our overconfidence-for-the-results villain. This coach will help you understand your current situation better and remove any confusion and uncertainty your team may be experiencing. It will also help you learn how to chart your own path towards your scientific thinking lifestyle.

Get Comfortable Feeling Uncomfortable

WE ALL HAVE DIFFERENT starting conditions, and while we each begin to pursue the scientific thinking lifestyle, we follow different paths to get there. Regardless of your industry, position, skill, or educational level, this coach is your personal mentor and guide.

It does not matter what field you are in. If you want to build a winning ecosystem, get comfortable with feeling uncomfortable because this coach will expand and challenge your thinking. Documenting your reflections after each chapter will enhance and deepen your thinking. What you are holding in your hands is your coach, and it will continue to influence you if you invest time in your reflections. If you follow your coach's lead, you will have instant breakthroughs that will allow you to serve your customers, employees, shareholders, family, and community better.

This coach will help you implement and practice continuous improvement in a system where Improvement and Coaching KATA, Training Within Industry, Lean 6σ, and data analysis coexist. At the end of each essential topic, I will reference the following:

1. *Toyota KATA Practice Guide* by Mike Rother.
2. *TWI Workbook* by Patrick Graupp and Robert J. Wrona.
3. *Understanding Variation: The key to managing chaos* and *Twenty things you need to know* by Dr. Donald J. Wheeler.

Before we begin our coaching sessions, I want to give you something that will allow you to trip over the truth every time you see it. Tripping over the truth is one of the ways we learn and expand our threshold of knowledge. Write the following pledge on a post-it and place it where you can see it every day:

I will make an immediate impact on myself, people, products, and processes if I believe the following:

#1: There is nothing arbitrary or unintentional about scientific thinking, especially when it comes to choosing goals and actions.

#2: No two individuals or processes have the same starting condition. This means I cannot copy and paste a solution to anyone or anything and expect it to stick.

This coach will help you understand how to take a best practice or corporate policy and turn it into a purposeful operational state. It will also help you focus on identifying and removing obstacles that prevent you from progressing. Only then will best practices adhere to our ecosystem.

Consider this question: Should you apply the same cure to a 65, 30, and 5-year-old suffering from the same virus? I hope your answer is no! Every individual or process has their own starting condition and obstacles. Make sure you fully understand this concept because it will open your eyes on everything you have been doing so far in your organization. Stop copying and pasting best practices even if corporate advances them. Instead, follow the coach's guidance, and you will implement them correctly. It is about the context, not the tools.

Why do you think your New Year's resolutions never really last more than a month? When was the last time you easily implemented best practices in your organization? Have you considered why? To address these questions, you must chart your own path towards the ideal state, and doing so requires devoting yourself to the scientific thinking lifestyle.

My Reflections Are

My Reflections Are

My Reflections Are

THE PURPOSE OF LIFE IS TO ENJOY EVERY MOMENT

Find Your Purpose

WHAT IS YOUR PURPOSE? Go ahead and write it below with a pencil – not a pen as you will begin evolving it.

As of Right Now, My Purpose Is...

_____

_____

_____

_____

_____

_____

_____

There is nothing arbitrary or unintentional about scientific thinking. How can you be a successful business person, parent, or friend without knowing and understanding your purpose? Before you can improve, you need to understand your starting condition. This coach reflects what I have learned and practiced regarding the scientific thinking lifestyle for over fifteen years. Instead of viewing the scientific thinking lifestyle as a journey, think of it as a way of life. Specifically, what you learn, you take with you wherever you go.

The only thing holding you back is your unwillingness to tap into the unknown part of your brain through scientific thinking. Just like booster rockets help space shuttles reach outer space, this coach is about to become your booster; it will propel you forward into the scientific thinking lifestyle.

Knowing what something is and how it works are essential ingredients for making changes and improvements. It is the why, however, that helps you engage people and begin charting your path through unknown territories. This coach represents the experiences I have had interacting with and coaching over 115 improvement teams. Its purpose is to help fill your abyss with knowledge and turn it into a manageable gap.

I am not your teacher on this road; I am your coach. You learn by practicing the steps yourself. The coaching you will receive is for teams struggling to make sense of how data analysis, Improvement and Coaching KATA, Training Within Industry, and Lean 6σ coexist within the scientific thinking lifestyle. The improvement tools are not important; rather, it is their link to scientific thinking that makes them impactful. If you and your team have a difficult time interpreting data without a statistician and expensive software, this coach will help you learn how.

If you have been exposed to the concept of Improvement and Coaching KATA and Training Within Industry and still struggle to understand their meaning, this coach will help you learn how. It does not matter what improvement system you have in place or how advanced your continuous improvement team is, this coach will challenge your status quo, develop competency at the deepest levels of your organization, and propel you forward to the scientific thinking lifestyle.

Who owns the improvement activities in your area or department? You and your team are. Keep an open mind and allow this coach to help influence your thinking from "work is the work" to "improving the work is the work, and it is fun." The concepts covered in the following chapters will help fill your abyss and allow you to begin practicing instantly.

In *Made to Stick*, the authors state: "The way to get people to care is to provide context. How do you get people interested in a topic? You point out a gap in their knowledge. But what if they lack so much knowledge that they have more of an abyss than a gap? In that case, you [have to] fill in enough knowledge to make the abyss into a gap. Knowledge gaps create interest. But to prove that knowledge gaps exist, it may be necessary to highlight some knowledge first. Here's what you know. Now, here's what you're missing" (Heath, 2008, pp. 91,92).

This coach will fill your abyss with knowledge if you continue to document your reflections.

The Dunning-Kruger Effect

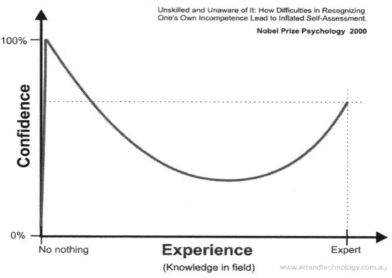

(Kruger & Dunning, 1999)

Figure 2: While Incompetent, We Think We're Great

EVERYONE, AT SOME POINT in their lives, has been a victim of the Dunning-Kruger effect. The DKE means we believe we know everything there is to know about a concept, but soon realize we do not. We try to devise reasons for our failure, i.e., we are unique; our culture is different; upper management is not supportive; anything to help us understand why something is not working for us. The bottom line is, we did not achieve our desired result. The relevant question is why?

When I began my continuous improvement journey in 2009, I thought I knew how the continuous improvement world worked. Indeed, I had read several books on the subject and was a Lean 6σ Green Belt. Additionally, I was a senior manufacturing engineer working with a leader who always made me feel like a million bucks. But after ten years of rigorous practice, observing other teams, and exposure to different industries, I realized I knew absolutely nothing. Somehow, along the way, I had missed the key-point.

It was not about the tools, or the storyboard, or the results. It was about purpose. Everything else was merely a component or side effect. When I finally understood this concept, I knew what I had to do to change my situation. In hindsight, I could have had more impact had I acknowledged what I did not know. After practicing in healthcare, manufacturing, financial and legal services for several years, I understood it was my way of thinking that mattered most, but only if it became a lifestyle. It is all about understanding your actual condition. Examining where you are is difficult for some because it may mean you need to change the way you do things. And, as most of us know, are resistant to change. Facing change is bold and requires courage! Let me share with you an example.

In 2009, my leader, Tom Robers, gave me a mass spectrometer operating manual. A mass spectrometer helps detect leaks on products. When he gave me the book, he said: "Panos, here is the manual, you got this." I eagerly jumped at the opportunity to learn something new. I read the manual, practiced on my own, received training from the equipment manufacturer, and rigorously began applying what I thought I knew. After several failures and miscalculations, and with Tom's continuous support, I soon felt like Rocky Balboa in Rocky IV! I discovered that if I wanted to make this piece of equipment work, I had to stop working from my own conclusions and begin working with a curiosity I had never experienced.

First, I had to identify my challenge. Then, I had to focus on grasping every detail of my current condition, from the actual working pattern steps to every behavior and attribute associated with it. I could not leave leaking helium bottles around the equipment because it could lead to false rejects. I also could not allow people to adjust the pass/fail settings just because they were not working correctly. Doing so could cause quality misses or excess rework. To address these concerns, I applied scientific thinking and removed obstacles faster than I could say mass spectrometer! This is how you will feel by the end of your first interaction with this coach.

How would you evolve your purpose now? Write it in the following reflection box.

Now, I Believe My Purpose Is...

_____

_____

_____

_____

_____

_____

_____

How does your purpose compare to the one you wrote at the beginning of this chapter?

My Reflections Are

My Reflections Are

My Reflections Are

EMPTY YOURSELF AND LET KNOWLEDGE FILL YOU

The Storyboard DNA

THE IMPROVEMENT STORYBOARD CAPTURES the four critical steps in an improvement journey:

Step 1 – Get the direction
Step 2 – Grasp the Current Condition
Step 3 – Establish the Next Target Condition and
Step 4 – Conduct Experiments

Figure 3 shows the storyboard layout we will review in detail in the following chapter. In Figures 4 and 5, an actual flow diagram helps guide you through the steps necessary to build your improvement storyboard. But, before we begin the improvement storyboard, I want to spend a little time helping you understand the Voice of the Process (VOP).

The VOP is a critical component of scientific thinking and impacts how you will address the four steps outlined above. If you do not understand what the data is telling you, you cannot expand your knowledge threshold. You will also need to familiarize yourself with the Process Behavior Charts (PBCs). In the Reference Materials, I give you a step-by-step example you can use to build your own charts.

Focus Process: Step 2a	Challenge: Step 1	
Target Condition Achieve by: _____	Current Condition	Experimenting Record
		Step 4b
Step 3	Step 2b	
		Obstacles
		Step 4a

Figure 3: Improvement Storyboard

There is nothing arbitrary or unintentional about scientific thinking. Once you have completed your reflections from the Reference Materials, please return to this chapter's next page.

Note: For more information on the Storyboard, please refer to Mike Rother's *The Toyota KATA Practice Guide*.

Let us reflect on what you know so far about the VOP:

What is your current condition? What is your actual condition? Do you understand the VOP? Yes ☐ No ☐

- If you selected No, please go back and reread the Reference Materials.
- If you selected Yes, show me your thinking. Let me see you build a behavior chart based on the following example:

Randomly select ten individuals and ask them to read the following paragraph and count how many times the letter "f" appears.

"These functional fuses have been developed after years of scientific investigation of electric phenomena, combined with the fruits of long experience on the part of the two investigators that have come forward with them for our meeting today."

Once you receive your responses, develop a PBC, and tell me whether the process is predictable. How can you tell? If you have any hesitation about your response, re-read the Reference Materials. Figures 4 and 5 provide a visual guide you can always reference in your path to thinking about your evolution.

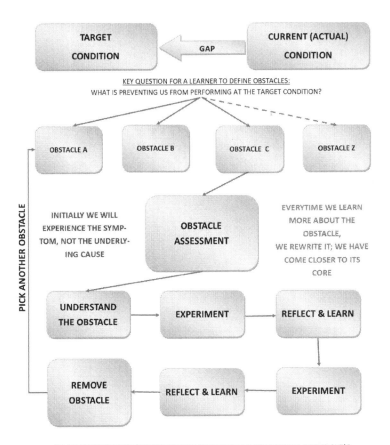

Figure 4: Improvement Process

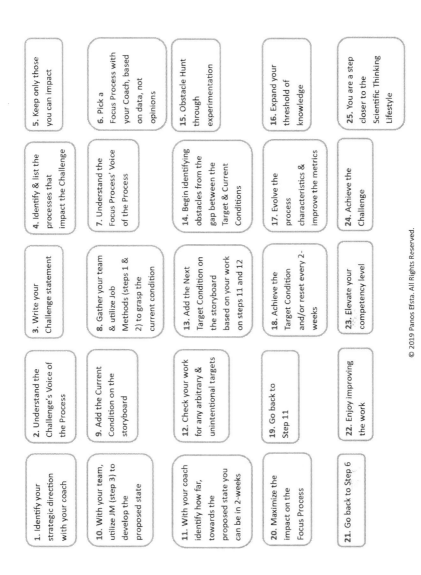

Figure 5: The Learner's Path to the Scientific Thinking Lifestyle

My Reflections Are

My Reflections Are

My Reflections Are

**DON'T LIMIT YOUR CHALLENGES
BUT CHALLENGE YOUR LIMITS**

Challenge Statement

Your challenge should directly correlate with your organization's strategic initiatives. Whether you use A3s, X-Matrix, or any form of Hoshin, you should align your organization's strategic direction with the challenge statement. Keep the challenge statement brief, focused, and exciting. Before you begin writing the challenge statement, you should first understand your data through the PBCs.

Pull at least ten baseline points from your process data sources and build your PBC of the challenge. What is the VOP telling you? Do you have a predictable or unpredictable process, and if so, how far from the Voice of the Client (VOC) is the process performing? Once you understand your VOP's initiative, write your challenge statement.

Example: *It would help make our patients trust that we deliver safe and quality care, and our employee confident on their abilities to serve our patients, if we achieve to reduce patient falls with harm and unassisted to 0 per year through our improvement work in the next 160 days.*

There is nothing arbitrary or unintentional about this statement.

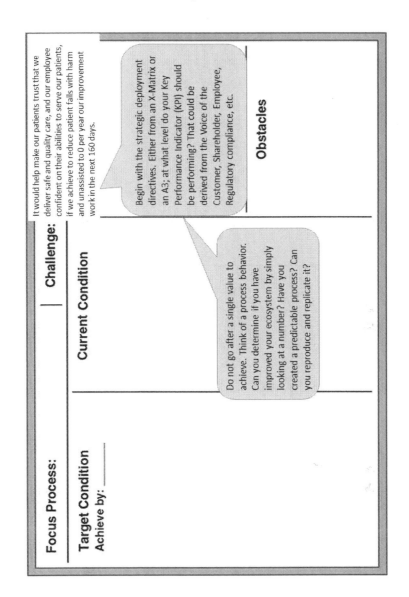

Figure 6: Challenge Statement

> *Coach's Reflection:* Always consider how your employees, customers and patients may feel about your challenge statement. Is it worded in a manner that creates excitement and passion? Is there anything arbitrary or unintentional about it?

Now, build your own challenge statement. Choose a strategic initiative, understand the VOP, and develop your challenge statement.

My Challenge Statement

_____

_____

_____

_____

_____

_____

_____

Note: For further information on the Challenge Statement, please refer to Mike Rother's *The Toyota KATA Practice Guide* – page 75.

My Reflections Are

My Reflections Are

My Reflections Are

_____

_____

_____

_____

_____

_____

_____

_____

_____

_____

_____

_____

_____

_____

_____

_____

_____

_____

_____

_____

_____

_____

THINK & ACT WITH INTENT

Focus Process

THE FOCUS PROCESS IS one of many processes that impact our challenge. Utilize your current value stream or process map to identify a narrow segment on which to focus. Make a list of the processes that affect your challenge. Review every process which you have identified with your coach and only keep those processes that you can fully or partially impact; remove any other from your list. Do not arbitrarily choose a process; instead, identify its starting (trigger) and ending points. You will need them in your next step (grasping the current condition through Job Methods). You may also consider your focus process as the "P" of your SIPOC diagram.

The Processes Affecting My Challenge Are:

_____

_____

_____

_____

_____

_____

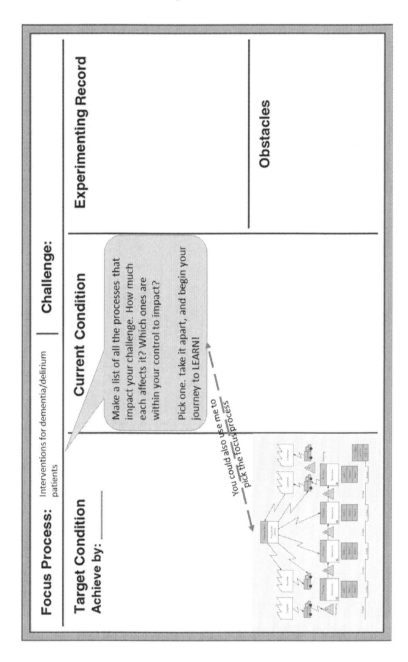

Figure 7: Focus Process

Take a moment to review your "pledge note." If you cannot find your pledge note, it is not close enough to you to remind you that: no two individuals or processes have the same starting condition. Once you have identified the chosen focus process, you then need to identify if that process takes place on different shifts.

If you read the Reference Materials, you understand that when analyzing the VOP, you should break down each process by shift, or individual when possible. Doing so will allow you to eliminate any unnecessary noise in your graphs that will force the limits to spread and hide any signals. Pull the data by shift, build the process behavior charts, and make your choice. Pick one process as the Focus Process (eventually we will address them all).

The focus process is not a desired state or target. If we cannot measure it, we cannot select it as a focus process. The focus process is the name of the specific process, i.e., *Scrub the Hub* (as part of the CLABSI reduction challenge) or *Developing the daily patient therapy visitation schedule* (as part of the Unable-to-see daily patient volume reduction challenge).

Example #1:

Here, you will expand on the challenge statement you created in the previous chapter. This is what you know from experience regarding processes that may impact the challenge:

Processes impacting the challenge:

    a) Bed alarm setup & utilization
    b) Tether alarm setup & utilization
    c) Patient room, chair alarm activation
    d) Patient education on fall prevention

e) Patient family education on fall prevention
f) Patient assessment completion during acceptance to med-surge
g) Patient shift intervention quality-completion by the RNs
h) Delusional patient shift intervention quality-completion
i) RN response to the alarm
j) Tech response to the alarm
k) Gait-belt utilization
l) Monitoring of delusional patients
m) Patient-mobility utilization post-surgery.

Before deciding which of the above processes to pick for the first focus process, you need to understand what the data is telling you. In this example, you pulled the data and found that in the last calendar year, you had 22 patient falls with harm in which the following occurred:

i. 12 are from patients falling from their patient room chairs
ii. 6 are from patients falling from their bed
iii. 2 are from patients falling during their walk
iv. 2 are from patient families present in the room
v. 11/12 chair falls associated with delusional patients

According to the above information, the team chose the process "h" as the first focus process. They chose the focus process based on scientific analysis, not arbitrarily.

Example #2:

This is what you know from experience regarding processes that may impact the challenge (we will review an example associated with CLABSIs):

Processes impacting the challenge:

a) Daily line utilization assessment by RN
b) Daily line utilization assessment review by MD
c) Completion of the CHG bath
d) Completion of the CHG shower
e) Quality of delivery of a CHG bath to a patient
f) Quality of delivery of a CHG shower to a patient
g) Scrubbing the hub
h) Changing of caps every Tuesday, Friday, and PRN
i) Dressing changes for the PICC at 7 days & PRN
j) Dressing changes for the implanted port at PRN
k) Dressing changes for the implanted port at 7 days with de-accessing & re-accessing of Huber needle
l) Dressing changes for the central line at 7 days & PRN
m) Verification of blood return & documentation
n) PICC Measurement at 7 days
o) Patient education on CHG bath necessity
p) Discharge education on CHG bath & soap usage
q) Addressing the quality of dressing
r) Placing alcohol disinfecting caps on all infusing lines
s) Assessing patient-with-lines transfers from other facilities
t) Patient with a line assessment upon admission to the unit.

Before deciding which of the above processes to pick for the first focus process, you needed to understand what the data was telling you. For this case, you pulled the data and found that in the last calendar year, the unit had 12 CLABSIs in which:

i.   7 were from patients transferred from other institutions
ii. 3 were from chemo patients with a port
iii. 2 were from patients the refused baths over 50% of their stay.

The team chose the process "s" as the first focus process. They made their choice based on scientific analysis. While your organization has unlimited goals, it has limited resources to meet them. Therefore, your organization should utilize the strategic deployment process to determine the challenge's desired outcome.

Strategic Objective	Patient Harm Events
Challenge Statement	Our patients will feel safer and more confident in our ability to deliver safe and quality care while our employees will become prouder for being part of our Med Surge unit, if we achieve to develop a <u>predictable process</u> with an Upper Natural Process Limit of 0.01 falls with harm per 1,000 Patient Days or no more than 1 fall with harm per year, through our process excellence work by 09/30/18.
Outcome metrics	i. Falls with Harm: UNPL = 0.01 per 1,000 Patient Days ii. Days-Between-Falls with Harm: LNPL = 365 days
Processes impacting the Challenge	a) Bed alarm setup & utilization b) Tether alarm setup & utilization c) Patient room, chair alarm activation d) Patient education on fall prevention e) Patient family education on fall prevention f) Patient assessment completion during acceptance to med-surge g) Patient shift intervention quality-completion by the RNs h) Delusional patient shift intervention quality-completion => Focus Process #1 i) RN response to the alarm j) Tech response to the alarm k) Gait-belt utilization l) Monitoring of delusional patients m) Patient-mobility utilization post-surgery
Baseline Data	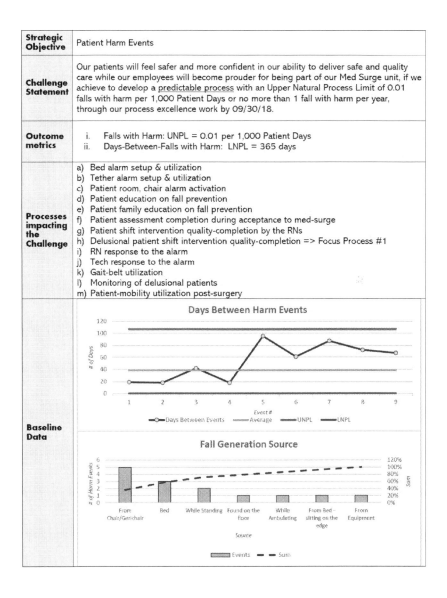

Figure 8: Example of Focus Process Analysis Report

Now follow the same steps and identify your focus process. Do not just arbitrarily choose a process but complete your analysis and let the data point you to the way.

My Choice of a Focus Process Is:

\
\
\
\
\
\

Note: For more information on the Focus Process, please refer to Mike Rother's *The Toyota KATA Practice Guide* – page 86.

My Reflections Are

_____

_____

_____

_____

_____

_____

_____

_____

_____

_____

_____

_____

_____

_____

_____

_____

_____

_____

_____

_____

_____

_____

_____

My Reflections Are

My Reflections Are

IMAGINE IF YOUR GPS CANNOT FIND YOUR CURRENT LOCATION. WOULD IT BE ABLE TO GIVE YOU ACCURATE DIRECTIONS TO YOUR DESTINATION?

Current Condition

THE FOLLOWING STEP, GRASPING the Current Condition, is one most practitioners fail to analyze in a way that allows them to overcome confirmation bias. If you base the current condition on your perception of how a process operates, that is known as an assumption. Any follow-up activities based on an assumption will result in stagnation. Eventually, improvement activity will become paralyzed, and the people involved will disconnect and give up on the scientific thinking method. It is essential to work with your teammates to use scientific thinking to investigate, analyze the data, and observe the process.

When trying to grasp the current condition of a new focus process, work with a team because you can observe and document the process details collectively. In other words, what one of you misses, another will catch, and vice versa. Altogether, you shall be able to paint a clear picture of how the process operates as of today, with all its variations and obstacles. During the process of grasping the current condition, we are looking for the specific working patterns that currently represents the focus process and all the behaviors and attributes which lead the process to perform the way it does.

Grasping the current condition through JM steps 1 and 2 allows you to strategically use the six questions to better understand the behaviors and attributes that interconnect every step of the focus process. You must make that connection with intent, following the sequence of the six questions – never deviating from them. Meanwhile, you are observing and interviewing those that work the process with the intent to extract valuable details and not to point to them that they are doing anything incorrectly.

Job Methods Six Questions from Step #2

1. *Why is this step necessary?*
2. *What is its purpose?*
   - *If it is not necessary or we cannot find a purpose for it, why do we even need to improve on it at the target condition, instead of focusing on removing it from our operation –*
3. *Where should this step take place?*
4. *When should this step take place?*
5. *Who is the best person to do this step?*
6. *How is the best way to do it?*

These JM questions help you think, plan, and act with intent. After you have identified the focus process, tell people in advance you will be observing them. Let them know you are not criticizing or assessing them, merely trying to understand the variation present in the focus process. Then, gather your team of observers and make them aware of what you will be observing. Where does the process begin (trigger point) and end? Once you have a clear understanding of the observation plan, go where the action takes place; spread your team around such that you all have a different point of view, and observe the process carefully. Focus on listening and seeing to understand. Gather all the details and begin asking the six JM questions in the sequence presented on the card. Try to grasp the current condition.

Note: For further information on the TWI Job Methods, refer to Patrick Graupp's *The TWI Workbook* – page 95.

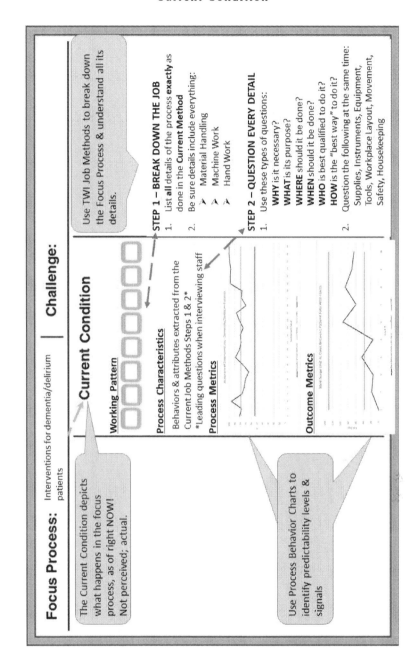

Figure 9: Grasping the Current Condition

Once you and your team have completed your observations, combine them, and lay out the current condition, as shown in Figure 10:

Working Pattern: The steps representing the Focus Process only, from its trigger (starting) point to its completion (ending) point.

Process Characteristics: Attributes of the working patterns, the linkage between each step as well as behaviors observed.

Process Metric(s): Process Behavior Chart(s) showcasing the performance of the Focus Process, correlating to the Outcome Metric(s).

Outcome Metric(s): Process Behavior Chart(s) showcasing the performance of the Challenge metric(s).

Coach's Reflection: Your focus process' current condition should not include anything derived from statements such as: I *think, I feel, I believe, I have a hunch.* The learner is responsible to update the current condition before each coaching cycle.

Note: For further information on the Current Condition, refer to Mike Rother's *The Toyota KATA Practice Guide* – page 89.

WORKING PATTERN

A. REPRESENTS THE STEPS THAT DESCRIBE THE FOCUS PROCESS AS OF TODAY THROUGH JOB METHODS (CURRENT METHOD)

B. UPDATE THIS CONDITION WITH THE MOST RECENT INFORMATION, BEFORE EVERY COACHING CYCLE.

PROCESS CHARACTERISTICS

A. BEHAVIORS/ATTRIBUTES THAT CREATE VARIATION IN THE WORKING PATTERN OR INTRODUCE POOR QUALITY, IN-FREQUENCY, OR VARIATION TO THE WORKING PATTERN—THOSE WE WISH TO ELIMINATE

B. THE JOB METHOD'S CURRENT STATE REMARKS

C. CAN BE NUMERICALLY QUANTIFIABLE (EX. CURRENT JOB INSTRUCTION TIMETABLE) - MEASURABLE BUT NOT AT SUCH A FREQUENT INTERVAL TO PLACE ON A PROCESS BEHAVIOR CHART

EX. HEALTHCARE: 75% OF ALL SHIFTS NURSES FOLLOW THEIR OWN INTERPRETATION OF THE C.DIFF CRITERIA

PROCESS METRICS (VOICE OF THE PROCESS)

A. ONLY REPRESENTS THE FOCUS PROCESS

B. NEEDS TO BE MEASURED DAILY ON A PROCESS BEHAVIOR CHART

C. UPDATE THIS CONDITION WITH THE MOST RECENT INFORMATION, BEFORE EVERY COACHING CYCLE.

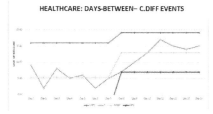

HEALTHCARE: DAYS-BETWEEN– C.DIFF EVENTS

OUTCOME METRICS (VOICE OF THE CUSTOMER)

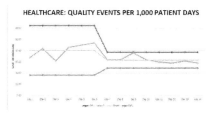

HEALTHCARE: QUALITY EVENTS PER 1,000 PATIENT DAYS

Figure 10: Current Condition Guiding Map

Often, teams ask: "how many different people or times should I observe the process to grasp my current condition?" I do not give them an arbitrary response because it is not part of the scientific thinking lifestyle. Instead, I tell them my favorite process is the Acceptable Quality Level (AQL) matrix (see Figure 11).

Organizations around the globe use the AQL matrix to inspect their products. If they cannot inspect 100% of their products, associates utilize such a process to determine how many they should inspect. The chart leads them to choose how many items they should inspect to be confident that if they found no issues in the initial sample size, then the remaining batch is defect-free. As shown in the table, if you have 60 employees and you want to be 99% confident that your sample size represents what would happen in your current condition, you should observe 13 randomly selected employees. It is your choice what confidence level you choose. This is also a great topic for the 1st coach to challenge you further. This is because the easiest thing to do is observe as many cases as possible. The question is whether observing as many cases as possible is effective? Will doing so give you a good depiction of what happens in your process today?

Figure 11: The AQL Matrix

Observation Size	90.00%	93.50%	96.00%	97.50%	98.50%	99.00%	99.35%	99.60%	99.75%	99.85%	99.90%	99.94%	99.96%	99.98%	99.99%	99.99%
1-8	2	2	3	5	ALL	ALL	ALL	ALL	ALL	ALL	ALL	ALL	ALL	ALL	ALL	ALL
9-15	2	2	3	5	8	13	ALL	ALL	ALL	ALL	ALL	ALL	ALL	ALL	ALL	ALL
16-25	2	3	3	5	8	13	20	ALL	ALL	ALL	ALL	ALL	ALL	ALL	ALL	ALL
26-50	2	5	5	5	8	13	20	32	ALL	ALL	ALL	ALL	ALL	ALL	ALL	ALL
51-90	4	5	6	7	8	13	20	32	50	80	ALL	ALL	ALL	ALL	ALL	ALL
91-150	5	6	7	11	12	13	20	32	50	80	125	ALL	ALL	ALL	ALL	ALL
151-280	6	7	10	13	19	20	20	32	50	80	125	200	315	ALL	ALL	ALL
281-500	7	9	11	16	21	29	47	48	50	80	125	200	315	500	800	ALL
501-1200	8	11	15	19	27	34	47	73	75	80	125	200	315	500	800	1250
1201-3200	9	13	18	23	35	42	53	73	116	120	125	200	315	500	800	1250
3201-10,000	9	15	22	29	38	50	68	86	116	189	192	200	315	500	800	1250
10,001-35,000	9	15	29	35	46	60	77	108	135	189	294	300	315	500	800	1250
35,001-150,000	9	15	29	40	56	74	96	123	170	218	294	476	490	500	800	1250
150,001-500,000	9	15	29	40	64	90	119	156	200	270	345	476	715	750	800	1250
500,001 & Over	9	15	29	40	64	102	143	189	244	303	435	556	715	1112	1200	1250

SAMPLE SIZE

There is nothing arbitrary and unintentional about scientific thinking.

Coach's Reflection: Have your team use Job Methods' six questions to grasp the focus process' current condition (coach, coworker, or even individuals from another department or location. Question every process detail with the intent to grasp the current condition. Follow the Job Methods' card steps 1 and 2.

Note: You can access online resources for more information about the AQL process.

My Reflections Are

My Reflections Are

My Reflections Are

EVERY TARGET IS A STEP TOWARDS A BETTER TOMORROW

Target Condition

Now that you have a comprehensive picture of the current condition, setting the target condition becomes easier because you used your scientific thinking skills. You are trying to develop your team's cognitive ability o they reach a competent level that allows them to utilize their creative mindset. JM's six questions let you form a robust working pattern with its associated behaviors and attributes. However, the proposed state you will develop with your team will be several target conditions away from you. The question you should be asking is: how close can you get to the proposed design-state in two-weeks? The answer to this question will help develop the next target condition. Similarly, if you have designed your desired working pattern, you can use the same process to break it down into incremental target conditions. The desired state is what you see several target conditions away. The target condition is the next stop.

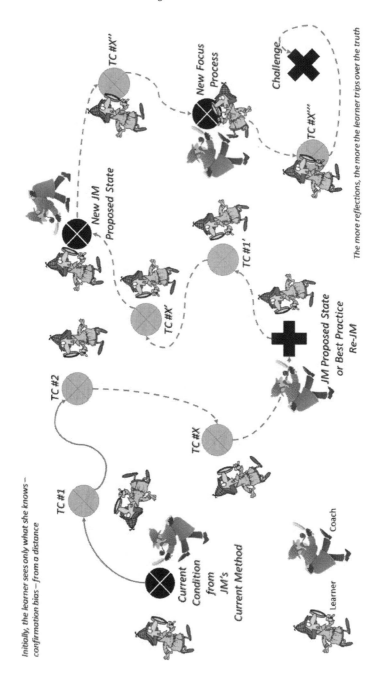

Figure 12: The Uncharted Territory Towards the Challenge

Focus Process: Interventions for dementia/delirium patients

Challenge:

Experimenting Record

Target Condition

Achieve by:

Working Pattern

Pinpoint/highlight which steps are different for this 2-week TC

Acting with intent!

Job Methods will help us develop a process layout that is several TCs ahead of us. We will make that our ideal state and for each TC we focus on coming closer to that ideal state.

Process Characteristics

Behaviors & attributes which support the TC working pattern

Process Metrics

4 Process Behavior Rules

Don't target one data point to reach but create a process signal

Outcome Metrics

What pattern is the targeted process metric going to cause - 4 Process Behavior Rules

This is not the Challenge's numerical goal, unless we are close to achieving it

STEP 3 – DEVELOP THE NEW METHOD

1. **ELIMINATE** unnecessary details
2. **COMBINE** details when practical
3. **REARRANGE** details for better sequence
4. **SIMPLIFY** all details

To make the job easier and safer to do:
- Put supplies, instruments & equipment into the **best position** and within **convenient reach** for the worker
- Use **gravity feed hoppers** or **drop delivery chutes** whenever possible
- Make effective use of **both hands**
- Use **holder or devices** instead of hands

5. Work out your ideas **WITH OTHERS**
6. **WRITE UP** the proposed new method

Obstacles

Figure 13: Developing the Next Target Condition

When dealing with a new focus process, use JM's step #3 with your team to identify the proposed state. Do not forget that during the observation stage, you asked these questions as part of your operator-interview process. Be specific; give information about how you should lay out the proposed process. The learner and 1st coach will pair to develop the next target condition. The 1st coach should be present during this step – especially during the beginning stages of a learner's exposure to scientific thinking. The 1st coach will assist you in avoiding arbitrary targets. Each target condition helps the learner expand her knowledge threshold. As a result, the process gets closer to the proposed state. Every target condition should be closer to the proposed state. If you achieve the proposed state and the process metric shows the focus process should be further improved before moving on to another one, the learner should go back and repeat the JM process with a different observation team. A different team will offer a fresh perspective on how the process could operate at a higher performance level. The proposed state helps keep the learner on course. **There is nothing arbitrary or unintentional about scientific thinking.**

WORKING PATTERN

A. THIS IS NOT THE JOB METHODS PROPOSED STATE BUT A PORTION OF IT

B. THE JOB METHOD'S PROPOSED STATE IS AT A FURTHER OUT TARGET CONDITION—BREAK THE PROPOSED STATE INTO TWO-WEEK TARGET CONDITIONS

PROCESS CHARACTERISTICS

A. BEHAVIORS/ATTRIBUTES THAT FACILITATE THE QUALITY OR FREQUENCY OF THE WORKING PATTERN—THOSE WE WISH TO DUPLICATE AND SPREAD FOR SUCCESS

B. BEHAVIORS/ATTRIBUTES THAT BREAK OR INTRODUCE POOR QUALITY, INFREQUENCY, OR VARIATION TO THE WORKING PATTERN—THOSE WE WISH TO ELIMINATE

C. CAN BE NUMERICALLY QUANTIFIABLE (EX. CURRENT JOB INSTRUCTION TIMETABLE)—CANNOT PUT ON A RUN CHART

EX. HEALTHCARE: WE HAVE DEVELOPED A JOB INSTRUCTION BREAKDOWN ON THE APPLICATION OF C.DIFF CRITERIA

PROCESS METRICS (VOICE OF THE PROCESS)

A. ONLY REPRESENTS THE FOCUS PROCESS. A PREDICTION OF HOW THE PROCESS IS BEHAVING BY THE TIME WE REACH THE TARGET DATE

B. DO NOT TRY TO PREDICT A NUMBER BUT A PROCESS BEHAVIOR (EX. X NUMBER OF POINTS ABOVE/BELOW THE MEAN, OR CREATION OF A SPECIFIC TYPE OF SIGNAL)

C. REPRESENTS A PREDICTION FOR ONLY THIS TARGET CONDITION CYCLE (2-WEEKS OUT)

EX. HEALTHCARE: 8 CONSECUTIVE POINTS ABOVE THE AVERAGE FOR THE DAYS-BETWEEN C.DIFF EVENTS

OUTCOME METRICS (VOICE OF THE CUSTOMER)

A. THE SAME METRICS AS THOSE STATED IN OUR CHALLENGE STATEMENT

B. PREDICTION OF HOW THE PROCESS IS BEHAVING BY THE TIME WE REACH THE TARGET CONDITION DATE (2-WEEKS)

C. DO NOT TRY TO PREDICT A NUMBER BUT A PROCESS BEHAVIOR (EX. X NUMBER OF POINTS ABOVE/BELOW THE MEAN)

REPRESENTS A PREDICTION FOR ONLY THIS TARGET CONDITION CYCLE (2-WEEKS OUT)

EX. HEALTHCARE: 1 POINT UNDER THE LNPL FOR THE QUALITY EVENTS PER 1,000 PATIENT DAYS

Figure 14: Target Condition Guiding Map

Coach's Reflection: The target condition should not have any arbitrary or unintentional targets in it. Once the coach and team has helped the learner develop the proposed state through JM, it is then the coach's responsibility to mentor and guide – **not tell** – the learner on how far she/he can go in the next two weeks. If you follow this process, you will help the learner reduce the gap between the chosen targets and what is actually achieved at the end of each target condition. The larger the gap, the slower the progress for both the learner and the improvement process.

Note: For further information on the Target Condition, you can refer to Mike Rother's *The Toyota KATA Practice Guide* – page 123.

My Reflections Are

My Reflections Are

My Reflections Are

> **OBSTACLES ARE LIKE A PATIENT. THEY NEED A THOROUGH EXAMINATION BEFORE ANY MEDICATION IS PRESCRIBED**

Obstacles

WHEN I WAS A kid, Road Runner was my favorite cartoon character. He was not only funny but ingenious. You will soon realize why. Fast forward to today, and the lessons I have learned throughout my career of "chasing the roadrunner" are priceless.

Let's think of the Road Runner as the Target Condition. The coyote could never catch the Road Runner because he had poor obstacle-hunting skills. The coyote focused on catching the Road Runner instead of assessing his obstacles. As hard as he tried, he always failed; he never learned. How many of us have been like the coyote? I know I have. Solutions-driven thinking is going to leave you hungry like the coyote. Obstacle-hunting is the approach you should follow and is the only way you will expand your knowledge threshold. Too bad the coyote did not have a coach to help him identify and pursue his purpose.

Obstacle-hunting is essential to identify what is keeping your focus process from operating at its next target condition. One critical step some often miss is that an outcome metric is just a side effect of the focus process. You will never associate an obstacle with it. You can never work directly to improve an outcome metric. Your focus should be on improving the current focus process – characteristics and metrics – which will help bring you closer to the challenge. The way you measure an obstacle should be part of your process metrics. You will find this factor essential when you try to connect each experiment's expectation to a process metric. You will soon find that the underlying reason why processes perform the way they do relates to behaviors and habits. Once you understand this, obstacle-hunting becomes methodical and effective. **There is nothing arbitrary and unintentional about scientific thinking.**

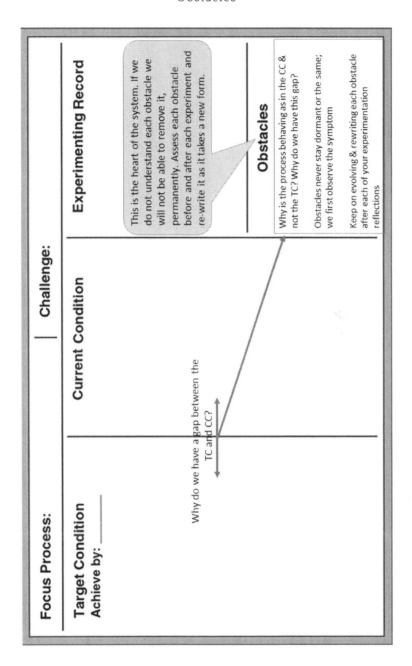

Figure 15: Obstacles

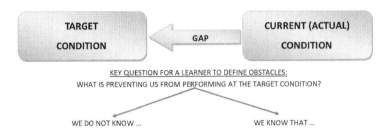

KEY QUESTION FOR A LEARNER TO DEFINE OBSTACLES:
WHAT IS PREVENTING US FROM PERFORMING AT THE TARGET CONDITION?

WE DO NOT KNOW ...   WE KNOW THAT ...

FACT

A. WHAT IS TRUE ABOUT THE OBSTACLE AS OF RIGHT NOW?

FIGURE/DATA

A. CAN WE ASSOCIATE ANY DATA WITH THE ABOVE FACT?

B. INSTEAD OF STATING "MANY" OR "A LOT" OR "UNDESIRED VARIATION" TRY QUANTIFYING IT.

NEGATIVE IMPACT

A. WHAT PART OF THE TARGET WORKING PATTERN IS THIS KEEPING US FROM ACCOMPLISHING?

B. WHAT IS THE PROCESS METRIC AFFECTED AND BY HOW MUCH?

PUTTING IT ALL TOGETHER

A. DESCRIBE THE OBSTACLE BY PUTTING TOGETHER THE FACT, FIGURE, & NEGATIVE IMPACT IN ONE DESCRIPTIVE
    SENTENCE

B. HOW CAN YOU MEASURE THE OBSTACLE'S MAGNITUDE, FREQUENCY, OR IMPACT ON THE TARGET WORKING
    PATTERN?

LINKING IT TO THE TARGET CONDITION

A. WHICH PROCESS CHARACTERISTIC DOES IT AFFECT & HOW? (FACT)

B. WHICH PROCESS METRIC DOES IT IMPACT & BY HOW MUCH? (NEGATIVE IMPACT)

EVOLUTION IN OUR THINKING

A. THE OBSTACLE WILL NEVER STAY THE SAME AS INITIALLY IDENTIFIED

B. EVERY EXPERIMENT HELPS US GET CLOSER TO THE DNA/ROOT OF THE OBSTACLE

C. THE INITIAL OBSTACLE LOOKS LIKE THE EFFECT/SYMPTOM AND NOT THE UNDERLYING CAUSE

EX. HEALTHCARE: THE VARIATION IN THE WAY STAFF INTERPRET THE C.DIFF CRITERIA DURING THE PATIENTS
OVERNIGHT STAY **CAUSES** 75% OF C.DIFF EVENTS TO BE MISSED WITHIN THE INITIAL WINDOW OF 72 HOURS,
RESULTING IN AN AVERAGE OF 34 DAYS BETWEEN C.DIFF EVENTS.

Figure 16: Obstacle-Hunting Map

How to Fill Out the Obstacle Form

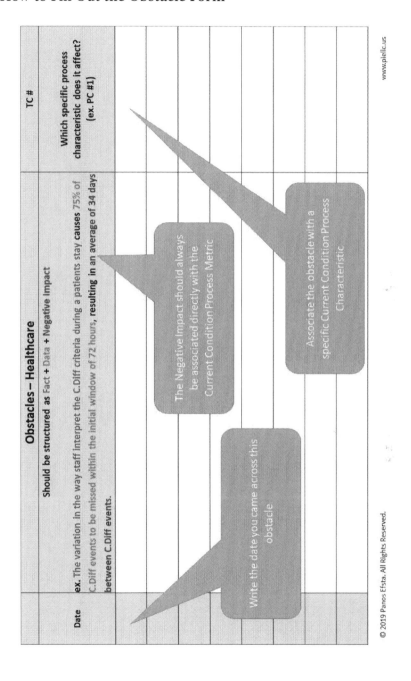

Coaching advice: Majority of the beginner-level learners will fall victims for one or more of the following four scenarios:

1. Pre-populates the obstacle form before the development of the Next Target Condition.
2. Does not evolve and re-write the obstacle: an obstacle cannot remain the same as you observed it initially. Each experimentation allows us to assess it better and come closer to its underlying cause?
3. Does not identify what specific process characteristic the obstacle is impacting.
4. Writes the obstacle without following the Facts + Data + Negative Impact layout.

Avoid these pitfalls by constantly reviewing the obstacles.

Coach's Reflection: The obstacles are the heart of the storyboard. Initially, a learner will confuse the symptom observed for the true obstacle. It is the responsibility of the 1st coach, to help guide the learner to identify the underlying causes behind the symptom and constantly updating the content of the obstacle written in the form.

Note: For further information on the Obstacles, you can refer to Mike Rother's *The Toyota KATA Practice Guide* – page 153.

Obstacles – Healthcare

Date		Should be structured as *Fact* + *Data* + *"Negative Impact"*	Which specific process characteristic does it affect? (ex. PC #1)
		ex. *The variation in the way staff interpret the C.Diff criteria during a patients stay* **causes** 75% of C.Diff events *to be missed within the initial window of 72 hours,* **resulting in "an average of 34 days between C.Diff events."**	
11/02/18		We do not know how big the variation is among our RN staff in the interpretation of the C.Diff criteria which causes us not to be able to pin-point the source of the deviation from our standard, and causing us to not be able to extent the days-between-C.Diff events beyond 34 days.	PC #2
11/04/18 – 1		100% of our freshman RN sample size observed, interpret the C.Diff criteria because they do not connect all the symptoms together, instead they have been reacting to one at a time and missing that the patients has C.Diff, resulting in our current condition performance of 34 days between C.Diff events.	PC #2
11/04/18 – 2		80% of our RN sample size observed, do not instantly connect and communicate with the on-call provider to proceed with additional testing, causing us to delay the patient quarantine, resulting in our current condition performance of 34 days between C.Diff events.	PC#2

www.pieflc.us

Figure 17: Obstacle Form

My Reflections Are

My Reflections Are

My Reflections Are

EXPERIMENT WITH THE INTENT TO LEARN, NOT JUST SOLVE THE PROBLEM

Experimentation

EVERY EXPERIMENT HELPS YOU better understand how to surmount an obstacle. Experiments are not about devising random ideas and seeing which one works. Experiments are about understanding what you are trying to solve and creating a robust solution that allows you to remove the obstacle permanently. There are five types of experiments, and all of them have a purpose.

Go & See: Collect data, interview employees, observe the process – you are not impacting the process.

Hypothesis: Change one factor only in the process – you could be impacting the process.

Exploratory: Change more than one factor in the process – you are impacting the process.

Job Instruction: Follow the 4-step process to train and validate your employees.

Job Relations: (Proactive) Invest in the four foundations to avoid spending time on conflict resolution. (Reactive) Conflict resolution through the 4-step process.

Experimenting Record

Coach the learner to experiment with the intent to first understand the obstacle and then remove it. Do not treat experimentation as an idea generation activity. Unless you understand the obstacle to identify and remove the underlying cause(s), you will not achieve or sustain the improvement. The obstacle removal will come only after we have assessed the obstacle and understood its core.

Go & See: Collect data & information, inquire opinions & facts, observe the process steps & characteristics. You are not impacting the process – (conduct multiple at a time or parallel to another type)

Hypothesis: Change one factor only and measure how that affects the overall process. Think of it as changing one ingredient in a recipe. You taste test it to check what happens. You could be impacting the process – (conduct one at a time)

Exploratory: Change more than one factors and measure how that affects the overall process. This is where you try running the process as intended to its target condition & see what you learn. This is where you develop and road-test a JIB. Think of it as changing one ingredient in a recipe, the cooking time, and size of the pan. You taste test it to check what happens. You are impacting the process – (conduct one at a time)

JI: Develop & deliver training by following the 4-step method – (conduct one at a time)

JR: Invest in the four foundations to build good employee relations and avoid spending time on conflict resolution; or institute an employee conflict resolution by following the 4-step method – (conduct multiple at a time)

Consecutive Go&Sees are a indication to the Coach that the learner is not learning or does not feel comfortable with experimentation

The more you invest in the Job Relations foundations, the less you spend on conflict resolution. Treat the former at your Roth IRA investment and the latter you income tax payment.

Figure 18: Experimentation

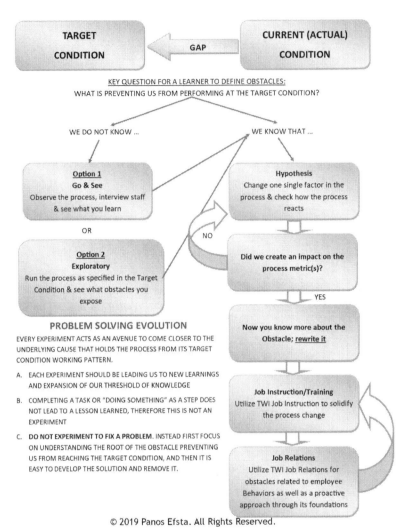

Figure 19: Experimentation Guiding Map

How to Fill Out the PDSA Form

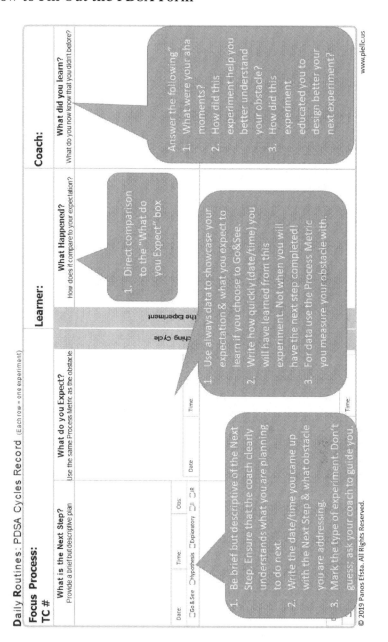

Daily Routines: PDSA Cycles Record (Each row = one experiment)

Focus Process: C.Diff Criteria Interpretation | **Learner: Kate** | **Coach: Panos**
TC # 4

What is the Next Step? Provide a brief but descriptive plan	What do you Expect? Use the same Process Metric as the obstacle	What Happened? How does it compare to your expectation?	What did you learn? What do you now know that you didn't before?
Because I don't know how big of a variation we have in the interpretation of the C.Diff criteria, I'll interview 10 RNs on each shift, after following them to understand what causes that variation Date: 11/03/18 · Time: 8:00 · Obs: 11/02/18 X Go & See ☐ Hypothesis ☐ Exploratory ☐ i ☐ R	1. Variation of how we communicate the information to the doctor 2. Several RNs not paying attention to the patient symptoms collectively—they don't paint the holistic picture accurately Date: 11/04/18 · Time: 8:00	1. 8/10 RNs interviewed do not prompt for additional testing (stool) because they believe the doctor knows everything about the patient 2. 5/5 freshman RNs interviewed react to each patient symptom individually, failing to make the connection to C.Diff.	While there is no pattern between shifts, it seems there is a clear pattern with newer nurses, as they all failed to connect all the symptoms. Meanwhile, majority of our staff experiences a disconnect with the providers at the expense of our patients. Not only do we have a variation in how we apply the standard but also struggle with how and when to communicate.
We will work with Dr. Anastasia, the unit's Head RN and Manager to develop a 5-step JIB which includes the communication to the on-call provider and follow up with road-testing with 2 of our newer RNs on days, and 2 on nights. Date: 11/04/18 · Time: 8:00 · Obs: 11/04/18-2 ☐ Go & See ☐ Hypothesis X Exploratory ☐ i ☐ R	100% of the nurses in the road-testing will be able to: 1. Accurately identify if a patient has C.Diff when the symptoms are provided to them, 2. Quarantine the patient within 2 minutes after symptoms are presented to them. Date: 11/05/18 · Time: 8:00		

(Band labels: Do a Coaching Cycle / Conduct the Experiment)

Figure 20: Example of a PDSA

Coaching advice: Most beginner learners will fall victim to one or more of the following scenarios:

1. Brief but not descriptive on the Next Step
2. No connection between the obstacle's negative impact (Process Metric) and the unit of measure in their expectation box.
3. Repeats the next step with their own set of expectations or states an arbitrary conclusion, i.e., I expect to train 3 people. The expectation connects with the Process Metric. In this example, the purpose of the training is to change someone's behavior and performance, not just train them.
4. Confuses "What did you learn" with what happened. What happened for the process is different from what I learned as a learner through this process.

In the beginning, a learner will set the experiment's expectations (What do you Expect? Box) arbitrarily, which can lead to a substantial gap with what happened (What happened? box). As you help develop the learner's competency, you will observe that gap getting smaller. That is a good indication that the learner is shifting away from arbitrary and unintentional predictions. Help the learner avoid these pitfalls by identifying your obstacles as a coach with developing her competency. **There is nothing arbitrary or unintentional about scientific thinking**.

Coach's Reflection: As we are changing how the process operates, we cannot forget the importance of letting employees know about changes that will affect them and develop the necessary training through TWI JI or any other method of your choice. We might even come across an obstacle related to an individual's behavior. We can experiment on all as part of our obstacle hunting mindset.

Note: For further information on Experimentation, you can refer to Mike Rother's *The Toyota KATA Practice Guide* – page 155.

My Reflections Are

My Reflections Are

My Reflections Are

THE PURPOSE OF LIFE IS TO KNOW YOUR-
SELF AND LOVE YOURSELF AND TRUST
YOURSELF TO BE YOURSELF

Target
Condition Reset

RESETTING THE TARGET CONDITION is essential as it allows you to gather your thoughts, reflect, and chart a new course of action. This reset takes place when you achieve all the elements of the Target Condition, or when the two weeks are up. Whichever comes first. As you evolve your thinking through rigorous practice, you will realize the importance that improving the work is not something we do once but throughout the day.

As we learned in the Target Condition chapter, setting each target is not linear. We first need to study our journey thus far and then determine how far to go next. Remember, the work we did through Job Methods allows us to have a clear direction. However, we are not in the process of breaking down each target to two-week intervals. Each time you ask yourself: *How far, towards the challenge, can I go in the following two weeks?* While we might not be able to reach every component of the target condition each time, we need to think through and understand what is important. The flow in Figures 21 and 22 give you a clear path to follow under each probable scenario. While similar, the one in Figure 22 differs at the final steps. However, as you develop your competency, you will begin making this process your own. Try keeping the reset process simple and minimize your paperwork. The storyboard is nothing more than a visual notepad. The thinking happens inside your brain and what matters the most is for everyone involved to learn and have enjoyed the process. **There is nothing arbitrary or unintentional about scientific thinking.**

IF WE MAINTAIN THE SAME FOCUS PROCESS

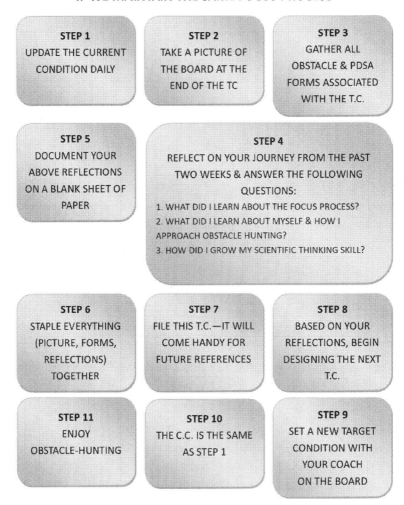

Figure 21: T.C. Reset – Same Focus Process

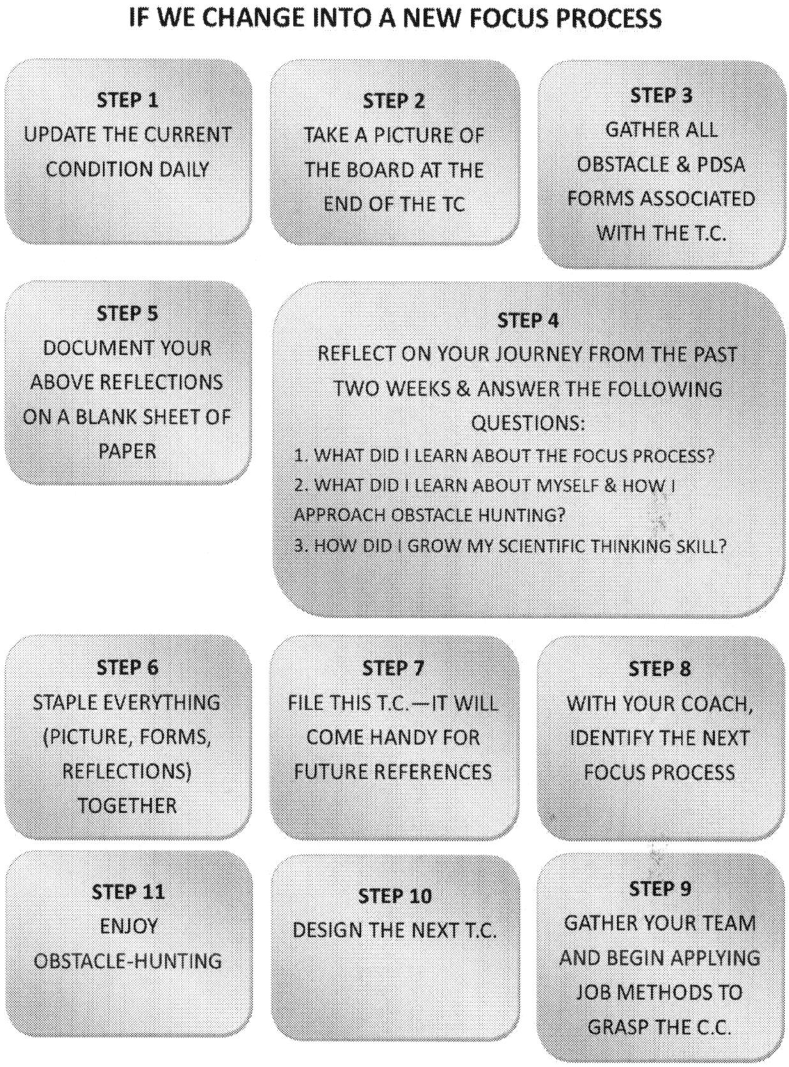

IF WE CHANGE INTO A NEW FOCUS PROCESS

STEP 1
UPDATE THE CURRENT CONDITION DAILY

STEP 2
TAKE A PICTURE OF THE BOARD AT THE END OF THE TC

STEP 3
GATHER ALL OBSTACLE & PDSA FORMS ASSOCIATED WITH THE T.C.

STEP 5
DOCUMENT YOUR ABOVE REFLECTIONS ON A BLANK SHEET OF PAPER

STEP 4
REFLECT ON YOUR JOURNEY FROM THE PAST TWO WEEKS & ANSWER THE FOLLOWING QUESTIONS:
1. WHAT DID I LEARN ABOUT THE FOCUS PROCESS?
2. WHAT DID I LEARN ABOUT MYSELF & HOW I APPROACH OBSTACLE HUNTING?
3. HOW DID I GROW MY SCIENTIFIC THINKING SKILL?

STEP 6
STAPLE EVERYTHING (PICTURE, FORMS, REFLECTIONS) TOGETHER

STEP 7
FILE THIS T.C.—IT WILL COME HANDY FOR FUTURE REFERENCES

STEP 8
WITH YOUR COACH, IDENTIFY THE NEXT FOCUS PROCESS

STEP 11
ENJOY OBSTACLE-HUNTING

STEP 10
DESIGN THE NEXT T.C.

STEP 9
GATHER YOUR TEAM AND BEGIN APPLYING JOB METHODS TO GRASP THE C.C.

Figure 22: T.C. Reset – New Focus Process

COMPLETED STORYBOARD EXAMPLE

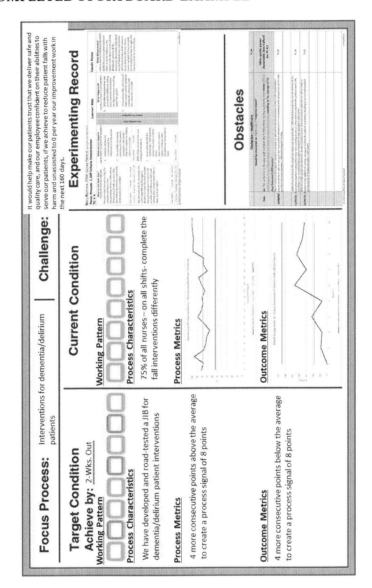

Figure 23: Healthcare Storyboard Sample

My Reflections Are

_____

_____

_____

_____

_____

_____

_____

_____

_____

_____

_____

_____

_____

_____

_____

_____

_____

_____

_____

_____

_____

_____

_____

My Reflections Are

My Reflections Are

LIMITLESS IS YOUR POTENTIAL

MAGNIFICENT IS YOUR FUTURE

Lean & 6σ

IF YOU OR YOUR organization are highly involved in Lean Six Sigma (LSS), it does not mean that KATA and TWI cannot work together in the same ecosystem. LLS has several tools you can use to better understand your process and innovate it. You could use the Failure Mode and Effect Analysis (FMEA), 5S, and even the lean wastes from your LSS toolbox, to grasp the characteristics associated with the current working pattern. Also, adding the TWI JI training matrix under the process characteristics will help you gain a good understanding of employee capability and competency levels associated with the focus process.

How about Overall Equipment Effectiveness (OEE) and Total Effective Equipment Performance (TEEP)? Both can act as the part of the challenge metric(s) an each of its components (Availability, Performance, Quality) broken down and approach as separate focus processes. There is nothing in your LSS system that prevents you from making it part of a storyboard. Also, ask yourself the following: is my data homogeneous? In this instance, homogenous means every data point has an identical background. For example, are all the patients in your length-of-stay tracking identical? If not, utilize process behavior charts instead of six-sigma-based control charts. Process behavior charts allow you to get a clear picture regardless of whether your data set is homogeneous or heterogeneous.

And how about 5S? When improving a process through KATA, we will need to ensure that employees know the current best way of doing the job. That is through TWI Job Instruction.

Within each important step of the Job Instruction Breakdown, we can add the 5S elements. As you see, every improvement tool in our toolbox fits within the scientific thinking lifestyle. **There is nothing arbitrary or unintentional about scientific thinking.**

Coach's Reflection: You can utilize your Lean Six Sigma tools as part of your performance innovation lifestyle. Use the tools necessary that help you understand the process and make them part of your improvement KATA storyboard. Be cautious when using six sigma charts when your data are not homogeneous. In any event, the Process Behavior Charts help us better identify and decode the Voice of the Process.

My Reflections Are

My Reflections Are

My Reflections Are

YOUR LEARNER IS YOUR STORYBOARD

The Foundations of Good Coaching

Coaching Assessment

Question: The images in Figure 24 are from actual coaching sessions with a learner and two coaches. What are the commonalities across all except one picture? (Hint: it is not the layout of the storyboard, number of people, or color – if you cannot find it or are uncertain, please write in the pre-assessment box "I DO NOT KNOW."

Figure 24: Your Learner is Your Storyboard

PRE-ASSESSMENT RESPONSE

(Before you proceed further in the book)

_____

_____

_____

_____

_____

_____

_____

POST-ASSESSMENT RESPONSE

(After you read the book)

_____

_____

_____

_____

_____

_____

_____

Coaching KATA

THE IMAGES IN THE previous assessment represent lessons I learned when I put the focus on the wrong storyboard. As you see, it is easy to get absorbed by numbers and forget that people matter most. Coaching is the hardest part of the scientific thinking lifestyle. You are responsible for molding an individual's thinking patterns, affecting the way they interact with others, and ultimately, their performance. As a coach, one must focus on developing a learner's skill-set and their lifelong habits.

One of the best ways to be an effective coach is by treating your learner as your child. Specifically, act with intention and always ask yourself: what is my purpose as a coach? Your answer should always be to build a winning team. Map the learner's journey from beginning to end and fill it with knowledge. Here is what we know and what we do not know. Below is an example that can help you visualize this concept. Your obstacle-hunting skill set allows you to begin turning the abyss into a "we do not know" gap, expanding the learner's knowledge threshold each time. **There is nothing arbitrary or unintentional about scientific thinking.**

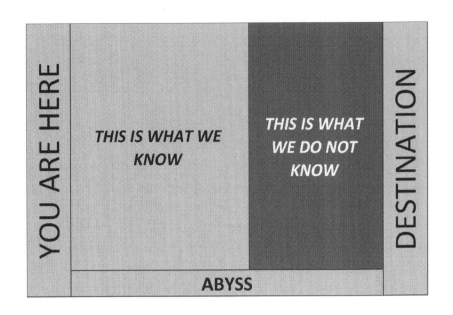

Figure 25: Filling the Learner's Abyss with Knowledge

My Reflections Are

My Reflections Are

My Reflections Are

WE ARE HERE TO SHOW LOVE, EMPATHY, AND PASSION

Staying in Character

THE COACH FOCUSES ON the learner's thinking, with a specific laser focus on the learner's brain; invests in the Job Relations foundations to reduce the risk and need for conflict resolution; utilizes the coaching KATA to access the learner's thinking, remove obstacles, and evolve it; coaches with love, empathy, and passion; constantly helps the learner to find and pursue her purpose, by listening and seeing to understand. The learner is the coach's reflection.

Coach's purpose: **Developing the learner is the work, and it is fun.**

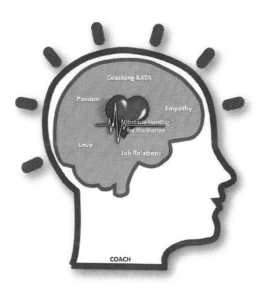

The learner focuses on the process while switching from problem-solving to obstacle-hunting mode; understands the Voice of the Process, grasps the process' current condition through Job Methods and evolves her thinking through the improvement KATA process; applies the Job Relations foundations to invest in creating a continuous improvement environment and Job Instruction to achieve standardization; constantly practices learning and expands the threshold of knowledge. The learner's perception of how things work is often far from reality.

Learner's purpose: **Improving the work is the work, and it is fun.**

My Reflections Are

My Reflections Are

My Reflections Are

EMPATHY IS ABOUT FINDING ECHOES OF ANOTHER PERSON IN YOURSELF

Guide the 1st Coach

THE COACH'S ROLE IS to help the learner identify and pursue her purpose through scientific thinking, making it part of her lifestyle. As a coach, my eyes and ears are on the learner, not the storyboard. My goal is to understand her thinking by coaching on and off the coaching card. This means I will follow the questions on the coaching card and determine the learner's goals by further probing her thoughts. Similarly, when you begin your process improvement journey, you will need to keep a constant practice mindset. This is particularly true at the beginning where it may take time to see a change in your performance data.

Scientific thinking is about infusing your ecosystem with a new way of understanding things and a different approach to innovation. The learner's development will help generate the process performance results you need to start building a performance improvement environment. How can I get the team (learner & coach) to activate their thinking beyond the five questions without robbing them of the opportunity to learn and grow?

Sometimes, coaches focus on the learner's storyboard instead of focusing on their purpose, development, and goals. Having been a coach and learner, I realized the learner should always face the storyboard, and the coach should face the learner, not the learner's storyboard. As a coach, you do not need to look at her storyboard to know whether she has any gaps in any part of the storyboard. Furthermore, as a 1st coach, when you hear the learner state "I think," "I feel," "I have a hunch," then you know there is uncertainty that will lead to arbitrary and unintentional work. As a coach, you listen and see to understand. Your ability to see to understand will reflect in the learner's ability to achieve the targeted performance results. As shown in Figures 26, the coaching card structure allows for several "help to understand your thinking moments." **There is nothing arbitrary or unintentional about scientific thinking**.

Note: For more information on the Coaching Card, please refer to Mike Rother's *The Toyota KATA Practice Guide*.

1st Coach to Learner

"Developing the Learner is my work, and it's fun!"

1) What is your purpose as a learner?

2) What is the challenge?

3) What is the focus process?

4) What is the target condition?

How did you choose each target?

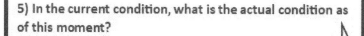

5) In the current condition, what is the actual condition as of this moment?

Let's review the last completed experiment

Flip me over to question A

6) What obstacles are now preventing this focus process from performing at its target condition?

7) Which one(s) are you addressing now?

Help me understand your choice(s)

8) What is the next designed experiment & what type is it?

Help me understand your choice of experiment(s)

9) What do you expect to happen?

10) How quickly can we review your reflections from this experiment?

11) How can I, as your coach, help you?

The Learner is Your Storyboard!

Figure 26-Front: Coach to Learner Coaching Card

A) What was the step you chose to take on your last completed experiment & what type was it?

B) What did you expect to happen?

C) What actually happened?

How does this compare to your expectation?

D) After reflecting upon this experiment, how did it help expand your threshold of knowledge?

Flip me over to question 6

TYPES OF EXPERIMENTS

Go & See: collect data & information; inquire opinions & facts; observe the process steps & characteristics. You don't change anything. (multiple at a time or parallel to another type)

Hypothesis: change <u>one</u> factor only and measure how that affects the overall process. Think of it as changing one ingredient in a recipe. You taste test it to check what happens. (one at a time)

Exploratory: change <u>more than one</u> factor and measure how that affects the overall process. Try running the process as intended to its target condition & see what you learn. Think of it as changing two ingredients in a recipe, the cooking time, and size of the pan. You taste test it to check what happens. (one at a time)

JI: develop the breakdown & deliver training by following the four TWI Job Instruction steps. (one at a time)

JR: Proactively build good employee relations by following the four TWI JR foundations; or institute an employee conflict resolution by following the four TWI Job Relation steps. (one at a time)

Learn more from us at www.piellc.us

Figure 26-Back: Coach to Learner Coaching Card

Obstacle Form – 1st Coach

Date	Obstacles – 1st Coach Should be structured as *Fact* + Data + "Negative Impact" ex. *The learner is inconsistent in the way she/he writes obstacles* which causes 50% of our coaching sessions interrupted and diverted in the development of that skillset, resulting in "50% of the coaching cycles taking over 50 min."	Learner's Name: What specific characteristic of the Learner's competency is it affecting? (Grasping the CC, Obstacle, or PDSA writing, etc.)

www.pielic.us

Coach's Reflection: The role of the 1st coach is to help the learner find and pursue her/his purpose, aligned with the principle of improving the work is the work and it is fun. As a coach identify the obstacles in the way of developing the learner's competency on scientific thinking. Complete your own experimentations on understanding and removing those. Authority is not coaching. Telling them what to do is not coaching. As a 1st coach, you are a learner as well; the learner is your storyboard. Position yourself to see to understand your storyboard. Pay attention to your learner and how she/he interacts with you through the coaching session. How comfortable are they? How easy it is for bias to guide her/his thinking?

Does this information trigger you to revisit your answer at the Coaching Assessment page?

My Reflections Are

My Reflections Are

My Reflections Are

COMPASSION CREATES UNDERSTANDING

Guide the 2nd Coach

THE SECOND COACH'S ROLE is to help the first coach identify and pursue her purpose by developing her coaching and mentoring abilities. A coach is not always an authority figure; she can be a learner, too. For example, the first coach is also a learner in the process of developing another learner. As such, we must ensure the first coach has the support, mentoring, and guidance needed to succeed. The second coach will help the first coach understand and implement excellent coaching skills daily. As a second coach, you should spend at least one session a week with your team (learner and coach) working through the second coaching card. Any signs of fidgeting, nervousness, and statements of "I think," "I feel," "I have a hunch" are indications of uncertainty that will lead to arbitrary and unintentional activities from the 1st coach.

The 2nd coaching card is an evolution of the 2nd coaching cycle, injected with the good coaching foundations influenced by the TWI Job Relations. You should devote your attention to the 1st coach only, providing feedback one-on-one. As a 2nd coach, praise publicly but always provide constructive feedback face-to-face in a private setting. You have a storyboard as well, the 1st coach standing in front of you. Therefore, you should always position yourself in such a way where you have a clear view of the 1st coach and the learner, observing the 1st coach's attention to the learner and their body language (see Figures 27). You are there to help develop a winning team. Therefore, observe the team dynamics and never interrupt the coaching session. Create a coaching binder with your obstacle and PDSA form and continue applying your scientific thinking. Follow the flow chart, as shown in Figure 29 to help you build a winning team. Do not rob the 1st coach of the opportunity to learn while coaching her/his learner. **There is nothing arbitrary or unintentional about scientific thinking.**

2nd Coach to 1st Coach

"Developing the 1st Coach is my work, and it's fun!"

1) What is your purpose as a 1st coach?

2) What is your Challenge & Focus Process for your learner?

3) What is the target competency for your Learner's skill development?

How did you choose that target?

4) Currently, what is the learner's actual competency level? *How can you tell?*

5) What was your last step? What did you expect? What actually happened? What did you learn about your learner? *One question at a time*

6) What obstacles are now preventing this learner from performing at the target competency level?

7) Which one are you addressing now? (1 only)

Help me understand your choice of obstacle

8) What is your next experiment as a 1st coach?

Help me understand your choice of next step

9) What do you expect the impact on the learner will be?

10) How can I, as your coach, help you?

The 1st Coach is Your Storyboard!

Figure 27-Front: 2nd Coach to Coach Coaching Card

FOUNDATIONS FOR GOOD COACHING

"Teach the 1st Coach one coaching foundation at a time"

Create a Purpose

⟹ Help the individual understand the purpose of coaching a learner—help build intent on the thinking and actions

Generate Passion

⟹ Energize the learner constantly

Promote Empathy & Love

⟹ Show respect for the individual

Let the Learner know how she/he is performing

⟹ Candor creates Trust & Transparency

Give Credit When Due

⟹ Praise the learner every time she/he learns

⟹ Do so when it happens, not later on

Tell the Learner in Advance of Changes that Will Affect her/him

⟹ Tell them why if possible

⟹ Work with them for a smooth transition

Make Best Use of Each Learner's Ability

⟹ Help the learner apply concepts without robbing her/him from the opportunity to learn

Learn more from us at www.piellc.us

Figure 27-Back: 2nd Coach to Coach Coaching Card

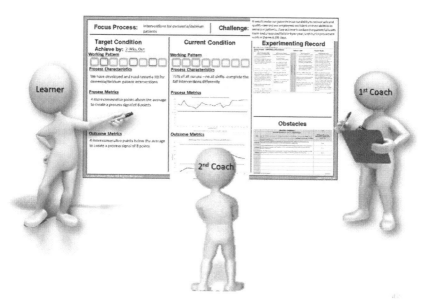

Figure 28: Recommended Physical Positioning
& Attention Direction of Roles

Obstacle Form – 2nd Coach

Date	Obstacles – 2nd Coach Should be structured as *Fact* + Data + "Negative Impact" ex. The coach tends to always focus on the storyboard, taking away his eyes from the learner, getting trapped in an idea generation discussion which causes the learner being at the advanced beginner level for the last 9 months, resulting in "no progression towards the challenge."	1ST Coach's Name: What specific characteristic of the 1st coach's competency is it affecting? (Good Coaching Relations)

Coach's Reflection: The 2nd coach's role is to help the 1st coach find and pursue her purpose. As a 2nd coach, identify the obstacles that stand in the way of developing the 1st coach's competency regarding scientific thinking. Bring them closer to the lifestyle. Complete your own experimentations on understanding and removing those obstacles. Authority is not coaching. Telling them what to do is not coaching. As a 2nd coach, you are a learner as well; the 1st coach is your storyboard. Position yourself to see to understand your storyboard. Pay attention to your coach – this is your storyboard – and how she/he interacts with learner through the coaching session, the application of good coaching foundations, and ability to mentor the learner without giving them any solutions.

Does this information trigger you to revisit your answer at the Coaching Assessment page?

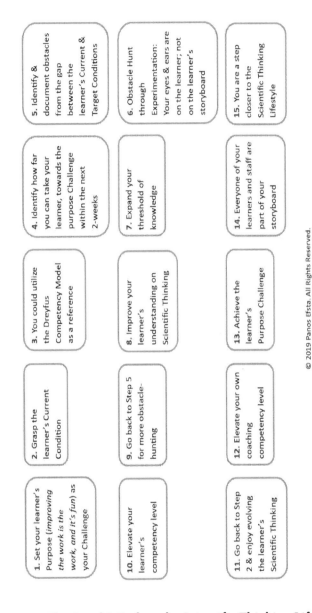

Figure 29: The Coach's Path to the Scientific Thinking Lifestyle

My Reflections Are

My Reflections Are

My Reflections Are

MAKE IT ALL ABOUT YOUR TEAM

Create a Guiding Coalition

A GUIDING COALITION IS an assembled team with enough power to influence, lead change, and encourage your ecosystem to work as a team (Kotter, 1996). To sustain your new scientific lifestyle, you need to create a guiding coalition that will focus on helping your performance improvement team pursue their purpose. The side-effect of such a coalition is going to be the achievement of all the different challenges you have on your storyboards. Purpose matters in everything you do and practice.

The individuals from your team who have practiced rigorously, understand the concepts I have shared with you thus far while being great stewards of change, now become members of the guiding coalition. Their mission is to help create winning teams (learner – 1st coach – 2nd coach), resulting in the constant progression towards their challenge. Each team will have obstacles that keep them from acting and performing like a winning team, but they are irrelevant to the team's storyboard. They are related to capacity development and team dynamics.

Jack Welch talks about putting the right players in the right roles, and TWI Job Relations states about making the best use of each person's ability. As a guiding coalition member, you are responsible for observing one or more teams and working with and for them. As a mentor in this capacity, your focus should be all about the team. Some questions to ask yourself regarding where to look for obstacles are:

(1) Is each member's purpose clearly defined and understood?

(2) Has the team practiced scientific thinking throughout the day?

(3) Is every team member learning and growing their skill set?

(4) Do they have the skills needed to advance toward their challenge?

(5) Are there good coaching relationships present?

(6) Does every member stay in character?

You, too, are a learner with a current and target condition, obstacles you need to identify, and experiments you should plan and execute to help build a winning team. First, you will need to create a visual dashboard where all your improvement activities, including those related to developing your TWI, KATA, Lean Six Sigma, VOP skill set, and any other initiatives necessary, are captured. Figure 30 shows you an example of how your dashboard could look, along with the essential components.

Once a week, the guiding coalition team should gather in front of their dashboards and work through a coaching cycle. Everyone should know every team members' initiative(s), so you can create an environment of trust and transparency. Each team member should play the role of the learner for their line of responsibility so that you continue to practice scientific thinking. I would recommend you that as a member of the guiding coalition to observe and assess – once a week – a team other than the one you are an actively participating as a learner, 1st or 2nd coach. Such a layout will allow you to develop your Job Relations skill set and put them to practice. **There is nothing arbitrary or unintentional about scientific thinking.**

Unit	Focus Area	KPI	Learner 1st Coach 2nd Coach With Competency Levels	Guiding Coalition Leader	Current Approach	Starting Condition	Challenge	TC Cycle	2-Week Target Condition	Actual Condition (As of Today)
Med Surge	Quality	Falls Per 1,000 Patient Days	Kate - Novice Panos - Advance Beginner Tom - Competent	Sara	Improvement KATA	12	Predictable Process UNPL: 1	3	8 consecutive points below current average	
ED	LOS	LOS – DC LOS – Admit	Panos - Advance Beginner Tom - Competent Chris - Competent	Brian	Improvement KATA	175 min. 123 min.	Predictable Processes UNPL: 125 min. & 80 min.	25	3 out of 4 points closer to the LNPL	
Hospital Wide	TWI Capability	# of Job Instruction Trainers # of Job Methods Trainees Level of Job Relations	Linda - Novice Dora - Competent James - Competent	Kim	Improvement KATA + Job Instruction	2 15 Directors'	15 40 Supervisors'	1	4 30 Managers'	2 15 Directors'
Hospital Wide	HR	Turnover	TJ - Advance Beginner Dora - Competent Tom - Competent	Lyndsey	Improvement KATA + Job Relations	32%	10%	9	3 out of 4 points closer to the LNPL	

Figure 30: Guiding Coalition Dashboard

Obstacle Form – Guiding Coalition Team Member

Date	Obstacles – Guiding Coalition Team Should be structured as *Fact* + *Data* + "Negative Impact" ex. *The team has been failing to focus on the skills development which causes* them to miss 4 out of the last 5 Target Conditions, *resulting in* "no progression towards the challenge."	Team: What specific characteristic of the team's effectiveness is it affecting? (Skill Development of Learner, 1st Coach, Good Relations, etc.)

www.piellc.us

Coach's Reflection: Your role as a member of the guiding coalition is to help create winning teams, spread the scientific thinking lifestyle, and be a steward of innovation. Make it all about your team, not their storyboard. Do not focus on the storyboard obstacles but identify what obstacles are holding your team back from practicing scientific thinking. The side effects of that are conflicts, performance deterioration, and eventually a dormant storyboard – where the team turns coaching sessions into group meetings. It is not the guiding coalition's dashboard that prevents any initiatives from going dormant but the discovery of purpose from everyone involved.

My Reflections Are

My Reflections Are

My Reflections Are

YOU ARE GOING TO UNVEIL
YOUR PURPOSE

Reflections

SCIENTIFIC THINKING IS NOT a project, initiative, or journey. It is a lifestyle that requires devotion, a willingness to learn, and an understanding that there is no such thing as failure if you are expanding your knowledge threshold. **There is nothing arbitrary or unintentional about scientific thinking.** You should not only expect yourself to apply scientific thinking at work. When scientific thinking becomes your lifestyle, you will find yourself applying it everywhere and with everyone around you.

Are you ready to begin charting your path to a new lifestyle? If so, take a moment to reread one chapter at a time and put it into practice. Reflect on the lessons learned and continue this process with every chapter. In so doing, your thinking will evolve, and you will achieve success in building winning teams. As we have reviewed, we initially pick a challenge that aligns with our organization's strategic direction (safety, quality, cost, delivery, etc.). Next, gather your challenge data and build the process behavior chart associated with your initiative. Try to understand the VOP (outcome metric) – the context behind the data. Ask yourself what processes impact that initiative? Make a list of those processes and identify which one can help make the most significant impact while allowing you to expand your knowledge threshold. Once you have picked the focus process, begin grasping the current condition by applying the JM process steps we discussed in chapter XI.

Spend some time observing the process with others– we are on seeing to understand mode. Focus on identifying and documenting details (behaviors, steps taken, movements, documentation used, interactions, communications, etc.), observing shifts, and watching people engage in the focus process. You should ask: how can I measure the way this process operates on a process behavior chart? Is the data available to me, or should I begin identifying ways to capture what I need? Begin building the focus process' process behavior chart(s) and correlate your team's observations with the VOP. What have you learned about the process? Do you feel confident you have grasped the focus process' current condition? Does your coach feel confident you have grasped the current condition? If yes, fantastic. Time to document it – document what? on your storyboard. If not, you should ask your coach for help and go back for more observations.

Once you have grasped the current condition, the learner and coach can use JM's six questions to begin developing the ideal condition. The ideal condition is several target conditions away from you. The six JM questions will help you develop a direction with intent. Once you have established an ideal working pattern, you should ask how much closer to the ideal pattern you can get by the next target condition? What process behaviors can you expect if you begin removing obstacles? That is your next target condition. Document it on your storyboard. Now that you have your target and current conditions ready, it is time for some obstacle-hunting. Use what you have learned so far to have fun experimenting, and never hesitate to challenge your knowledge threshold as a learner and coach. You will never stop having a storyboard. This coach has shown you how to plant the seed of scientific thinking. What you harvest depends on your devotion to the process of continuous practice, reflection, and knowledge expansion. Here is your challenge:

Now that you have finished your first interaction with this coach go back and reread one chapter at a time and begin practicing. See what you learn from reading and practicing. We all have different starting conditions, so you will have to address your specific obstacles as you chart your own path. Your coach helps you develop the insight and skill needed to begin creating the eco-system within everything that co-exists. It is up to you to learn, apply, and eventually evolve all the concepts presented here. Do not try to evolve a concept before fully understanding it.

The scientific lifestyle is the same regardless of the tools and systems you put in place. These are just components of it. Your harvest time is not far out. Are you ready to plant your scientific thinking seed? Get comfortable being uncomfortable. That is when you truly expand your knowledge threshold. When you began interacting with this coach, the first sentence in the Finding Your Purpose chapter asked you to write your purpose. Rewrite it now that you have exposed yourself to the principles presented so far. Take a few minutes to compare what you wrote before, and reflect on what you have learned? **There is nothing arbitrary or unintentional about scientific thinking**.

Coach's Reflection: No two processes or individuals have the same starting condition. While the direction might be identical, the path for each will be different. Each has its own set of obstacles in the way to the individual target condition. Do not try to experiment toward your target condition, instead, try to understand the underlying causes of your obstacles and remove them. Enjoy your obstacle-hunting and never take your eyes away from what is truly important: pursuing your purpose.

Please go back to the Coaching Assessment page, look at the corkboard images, and answer the question in the post-assessment box this time. If your pre and post-assessment answers are not different, I have failed you as a coach.

My Reflections Are

My Reflections Are

My Reflections Are

RECOGNIZE THAT YOU ARE CAPABLE

Reference Materials

The following pages were prepared to assist you in your capacity to understand data analysis. The details on the development of the Process Behavior Charts are derived from Dr. Donald Wheeler's *Understanding Variation: The Key to Managing Chaos.*

Make full use of these reference materials which are essential to your ability to build a robust storyboard and correlated your improvement activities with your process data.

Constantly practice the concepts presented from this COACH to help you build new and innovative habits THAT WILL HELP YOU DEVELOP WINNING PERFORMANCE INNOVATION TEAMS.

Simplified Data
Analysis

UNDERSTANDING STATISTICS IS NOT easy. Often, you will feel confused and overwhelmed. If you do not understand the VOP, you will not be able to correlate improvements with results. In this instance, context matters more than data. Your focus should be on insight, not numbers. Interpreting a process' performance by looking at a single data point or trend line is not effective. You should understand what, when, where, and why something is happening. You want to be able to conclude if something special is happening with your process and how far off you are from meeting the VOC. The Process Behavior Chart, an advanced form of a run-chart, is an innovative way to plot data and depict when the process communicates to you through signals or noise.

A signal is an indication of a special event that causes the process to perform unpredictably. When a signal is present, it is because something caused it. It is your job to find out what caused the signal. Noise is nothing more than common variation, but, it has its value when it comes to improving the process. Typically, the standard interpretation of our current run and bar-charts has been that some days we perform better than others. If you want to improve the process, you need to challenge your mindset and begin thinking differently. Your first step is to understand the behaviors and patterns that the data reveals through the process behavior charts.

Coach's Reflection: If you are using run charts and trendlines, you do not currently understand the Voice of the Process. This part is critical for you to grasp, as process behavior charts will change the way you perceive improvements and when you call an improvement, successful. If the process had a voice, what would it tell you? Pick up the process behavior charts and listen to understand.

Understand the Basic Calculations

To understand the basic calculations, you first need to know how to calculate the mean (average) and moving range (mR). You also need to understand the difference between the mean and median values. If you are using the median values, be prepared to switch your thinking. In your organization, there are likely key performance indicators that are captured with daily mean values and median values. We will explore those options, so you can understand them.

A mean is a number expressing the center in a dataset, and you calculate it by dividing the sum of the values in that dataset by the total number of values. The median is the middle value in the dataset. To find the median, list all the numbers in numerical order from smallest to largest, then pick the number in the middle.

If you have an even number of values, then the median is the mean value of the two middle numbers. The mR is another essential building block for the process behavior charts because it is a factor in the calculation of the process behavior limits. Let us look at the examples below and put theory into practice.

Mean Calculation (x-bar)

#	1	2	3	4	5	6	7	8	9	10	Calcula-tion
Mean	10	15	10	20	25	5	10	15	20	10	*14*

Figure A-1

To calculate the mean, first add all the values and then divide by the total number of values from your chart: x-bar = (10+15+10+20+25+5+10+15+20+10)/10 = 14. As you can see, all the numbers in our range will affect the calculated value of the mean. Therefore, if our process creates spikes or large drops, that will affect the calculated mean value by increasing or decreasing it. You want to capture those data points because they are part of your process' behavior. Using Excel, choose a cell, and type =Average (Data Range). Example: =Average(D1:D20).

Median Calculation – Even Number of Data

#	1	2	3	4	5	6	7	8	9	10	Calcula-tion
Values	10	15	10	20	25	5	10	15	20	10	
Median	5	10	10	10	10	15	15	20	20	25	*12.5*

Figure A-2

As shown in Figure A-2, after you identify each value, place them in numerical order, and identify the middle number. In this case, because you have an even number of values (10), the middle number falls between 10 and 15. In this case, we calculate the median by calculating the mean between those two values: (10+15)/2 = 12.5.

Median Calculation – Odd Number of Data

#	1	2	3	4	5	6	7	8	9	Calcula-tion
Values	10	15	10	20	25	5	10	15	20	
Median	5	10	10	10	15	15	20	20	25	*15*

Figure A-3

The example in Figure A-3 contains only 9 data points; therefore, the median value for that dataset after putting the numbers in order is 15. When utilizing the median calculation, ignore any extreme values in your data set. For example, if we replace the value 25 in the above table with 10,000, the median value remains the same, 15. If 10,000,000 represents your process behavior, you want to capture it, not ignore it. That is why you will avoid using median values. Using Excel, choose a cell, and type =Median(Data Range). Example: =Median(D1:D20).

> *Coach's Reflection:* Choose wisely when pulling your daily process performance data because choosing the median values could hinder you from exposing the actual process behavior. It is up to you to recognize the underlying causes that create spikes in your performance and how to incorporate those in your data set. Steer away from using median values and use actual or mean values to develop charts that depict your true process behavior.

Moving Range (mR)

#	1	2	3	4	5	6	7	8	9	10	Calcu-lation
Values	10	15	10	20	25	5	10	15	20	10	
mR		5	5	10	5	20	5	5	5	10	*5*

Figure A-4

Another important calculation is the mR which showcases the variation between two consecutive values in the form of an absolute value. To calculate the mR, subtract two consecutive values and then take the absolute value of that result. Another way to think of it is to subtract the smallest from the higher of two consecutive values. The mR is always a positive number. As shown in Figure A-4, the difference between each consecutive data set is calculated as: $|10-15| = |-5| = 5$ or $(15-10) = 5$. Using Excel, choose a cell, and type =ABS(Cell 1 – Cell 2). Example: =ABS(D2-D3). You will note the importance of using the mean values instead of the median, as the mR will reveal any violent shifts in the data.

Coach's Reflection: It is your choice to utilize any means available to you, to help you complete the above calculations. I am a big fan of what Excel has to offer, but I do not wish to limit your options.

My Reflections Are

My Reflections Are

My Reflections Are

Build a Process Behavior Chart

BEFORE YOU BEGIN DEVELOPING the graphical representation of your data, it is imperative to note a few essential factors. The charts are only as good as the data available. Therefore, you should always be aware of the quality of your data sources. When you have the data set ready, follow the steps depicted in the section Understanding the Basic Calculations, and prepare to build your process behavior charts. The fun starts now! Following, you will go through the six steps to help you develop the process behavior chart.

STEP 1: *Plot the data*

A run chart is a graph that displays the observed values of a variable (unit of measure) in a time sequence (days, weeks, months, etc.). Table A shows the daily volume of customers served by your organization, and Figure 5 shows the same volume of customers plotted on a run chart.

Day	1	2	3	4	5	6	7	8	9	10
Customers Served	83	87	91	86	87	90	91	88	87	89

Table A: Dataset

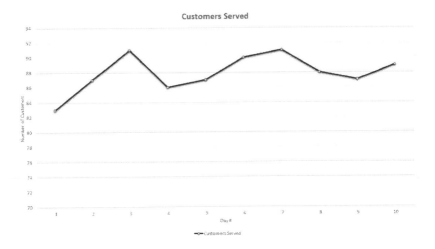

Figure A-5: Run Chart

In the first ten days of operation, we served between 83 and up to 91 customers. On average, that is 87.9 (~88) customers daily. Is that enough information to let us determine how well we are performing? What if we look at the trend line shown in Figure A-6? It seems we have been increasing our customer volume since day 1.

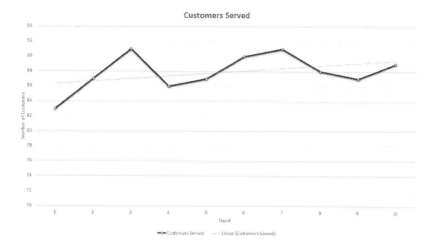

Figure A-6: Run Chart with a linear trend line

Does the above graph clearly depict whether we have improved the process? The trendline seems to indicate that we have improved, doesn't it? As we continue our journey on developing the process behavior chart, we will refer to this chart to answer that question.

STEP 2: *Add the Mean line*

Based on our mean calculation, Table A indicates we have served 87.9 customers. If you add the mean line, your chart will look like Figure A-7. This difference means "some days are better than others."

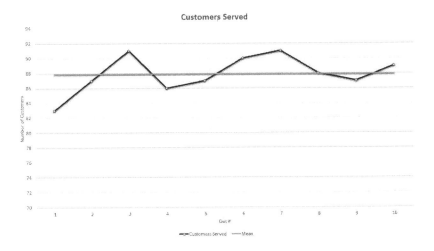

Figure A-7: Run chart with the mean line

STEP 3: *Calculate the Natural Process Limits*

In this step, we utilize the mean mR (XmR) calculation for our data set. Refer to Table A and then add the mR values.

Day	1	2	3	4	5	6	7	8	9	10
Customers Served	83	87	91	86	87	90	91	88	87	89
mR		4	4	5	1	3	1	3	1	2

Table B: Moving Range table

Calculating the natural process limits requires us first to calculate the XmR. Following the mR calculation process we reviewed earlier, you can see that the mean value for the mR is 2.7 customers served. Now that you have all your calculations in order, you will calculate the Upper Natural Process Limit (UNPL) and Lower Natural Process Limit (LNPL).

UNPL: (Mean value of our dataset) + 2.66 x (Mean value of the mR) which in our example equals: UNPL = 87.9 + 2.66 x 2.7 = 95

LNPL: (Mean value of our dataset) − 2.66 x (Mean value of the mR) which in our example equals: LNPL = 87.9 − 2.66 x 2.7 = 81

Note: the 2.66 factor derives from Dr. Wheeler's book where he goes into further detail about calculating this constant. However, know this factor is derived is not necessary for us at this point.

STEP 4: *Add the Natural Process Limits*

When you add the Upper and Lower Natural Process Limits to our run chart, along with the mean of our dataset, you get the graph depicted in Figure A-8.

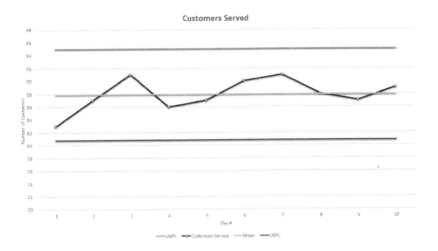

Figure A-8: Process Behavior Chart

Note: For further information on Process Behavior Charts, you can refer to Dr. Donald J. Wheeler's *Twenty Things You Need to Know* – page 23.

My Reflections Are

My Reflections Are

My Reflections Are

Chart Interpretation

CHART INTERPRETATION SHOULD BE as simple as possible to ensure everyone can build and interpret a process behavior chart. There are four rules you should have in mind when you are looking at a process behavior chart. These rules will help you separate noise from signals. Think of it as your heart rate. After an hour on the treadmill, your heart operates at a much higher level than usual. If you were to measure your heart rate after a workout and plot it on the chart, you would most likely observe a signal indicating something special is happening. I will expose you to a reference card that you can print and utilize when trying to interpret a chart. Do not try to memorize concepts. Try to learn to apply the concepts.

RULE 1: Any data point outside of the Natural Process Limits (Upper or Lower) is a signal that something special is happening and the process is acting unpredictably. When this signal is present, you call the process unpredictable.

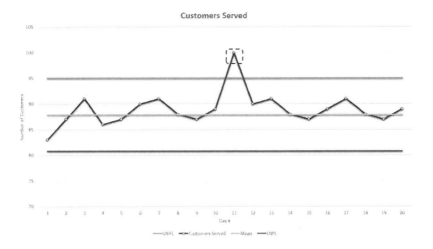

Figure A-9a: Process Behavior Chart with Rule 1

RULE 2: Eight consecutive points on either side of the mean indicates a signal that something special is happening and the process is acting unpredictably. When this signal is present, you call the process unpredictable.

Figure A-9b: Process Behavior Chart with Rule 2

RULE 3: If three out of four consecutive points are closer to either side of the Natural Process Limits (Upper or Lower), then the mean line indicates a signal that something special is happening and the process is acting unpredictably. When this signal is present, you call the process unpredictable.

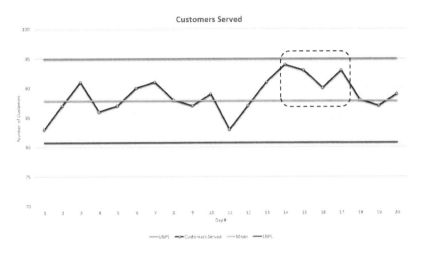

Figure A-9c: Process Behavior Chart with Rule 3

RULE 4: If none of the above rules are present, nothing special is happening and therefore, you observe normal variation or noise, indicating that the process is acting predictably. When this is happening, you call the process predictable. DO NOT WASTE time trying to explain or question any of the points on the graph.

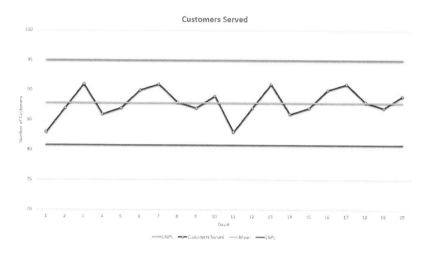

Figure A-9d: Process Behavior Chart with Rule 4*

The above rules are critical to the interpretation of your process behavior chart. The first three rules call for an investigation of the signals and identification of the obstacles that created them. Rule 4 indicates there is no need for any action if the VOP aligns perfectly with the VOC. Otherwise, the process calls for a complete overhaul if you want to change its behavior. Often, you have data sets that fall into rule 4 and waste time trying to interpret the noise. Other times you fail to treat signals as a priority and miss the opportunity to understand your obstacles. Avoid making these mistakes.

As you continue to collect your daily performance data, add it to your process behavior chart without recalculating your baseline data (mean and limits). The first ten days give us a good representation of how the process behaves, assuming no process changes have taken place during that time. Following, we will go through four case scenarios showing what the graphs will look like if we have any of the four interpretation rules present.

As indicated earlier, you can utilize the card in Figure A-10 as a quick reference to interpreting data.

Note: For further information on Process Behavior Charts, you can refer to Dr. Donald J. Wheeler's *Understanding Variation: The Key to Managing Chaos* – page 33.

Applies to	Rule #	Description	What is It?	What does it mean?	Reflection	Method to use
mR Chart	1	A data point outside of any of the Natural Process Limits: The process is unpredictable	Signal	Did you cause it through an attempt to learn or improve the process?	If the signal was caused as an outcome of your experimentation, reflect on what you have learned.	Improvement KATA
	2	8 consecutive points on either side of the mean: The process is unpredictable	Signal			
	3	3 out of 4 consecutive points closer to either side of the Natural Process Limits than the mean: The process is unpredictable	Signal	If not, it is a sign of instability in the process.	If the signal was caused from anything but your attempt to learn or improve the process, it requires you to further investigate.	Job Methods
Process Behavior Chart	4	None of the above rules: The process is predictable	Noise	Nothing special is happening	Begin experimenting (hypothesis, exploratory) and try to generate a signal that shows your experimentation is impacting the process	Improvement KATA

Figure A-10: Process Behavior Interpretation Card

185

My Reflections Are

My Reflections Are

My Reflections Are

How to Create a
Chart Using Excel

PUT TOGETHER A PROCESS behavior chart utilizing Excel to showcase the process' simplicity.

STEP 1: Gather your data, as shown below in Figure A-11a.

Time Interval	Unit of Measure
Day 1	17
Day 2	24
Day 3	12
Day 4	13
Day 5	13
Day 6	17
Day 7	22
Day 8	15
Day 9	14
Day 10	18
Day 11	19
Day 12	21
Day 13	16
Day 14	23
Day 15	22
Day 16	16
Day 17	22
Day 18	14
Day 19	16

Figure A-11a: Sample Dataset

STEP 2: Calculate the mean value, as shown below in Figure A-11b. *Note* the addition of the $ sign before each letter and number in the equation. The dollar sign is there to ensure we are only calculating the mean of the selection.

	A	B	C	D
1	Time Interval	Unit of Measure	Mean	
2	Day 1	17	=AVERAGE($B$2:$B$20)	
3	Day 2	24		
4	Day 3	12		
5	Day 4	13		
6	Day 5	13		
7	Day 6	17		
8	Day 7	22		
9	Day 8	15		
10	Day 9	14		
11	Day 10	18		
12	Day 11	19		
13	Day 12	21		
14	Day 13	16		
15	Day 14	23		
16	Day 15	22		
17	Day 16	16		
18	Day 17	22		
19	Day 18	14		
20	Day 19	16		

Figure A-11b: Calculating the Mean Value

STEP 3: Drag the calculated cell down to match the dataset selection, as shown in Figure A-11c.

	A	B	C
1	Time Interval	Unit of Measure	Mean
2	Day 1	17	17.57895
3	Day 2	24	
4	Day 3	12	
5	Day 4	13	
6	Day 5	13	
7	Day 6	17	
8	Day 7	22	
9	Day 8	15	
10	Day 9	14	
11	Day 10	18	
12	Day 11	19	
13	Day 12	21	
14	Day 13	16	
15	Day 14	23	
16	Day 15	22	
17	Day 16	16	
18	Day 17	22	
19	Day 18	14	
20	Day 19	16	

	A	B	C
1	Time Interval	Unit of Measure	Mean
2	Day 1	17	17.57895
3	Day 2	24	17.57895
4	Day 3	12	17.57895
5	Day 4	13	17.57895
6	Day 5	13	17.57895
7	Day 6	17	17.57895
8	Day 7	22	17.57895
9	Day 8	15	17.57895
10	Day 9	14	17.57895
11	Day 10	18	17.57895
12	Day 11	19	17.57895
13	Day 12	21	17.57895
14	Day 13	16	17.57895
15	Day 14	23	17.57895
16	Day 15	22	17.57895
17	Day 16	16	17.57895
18	Day 17	22	17.57895
19	Day 18	14	17.57895
20	Day 19	16	17.57895

Figure A-11c: Creating the Mean Dataset

STEP 4: Reduce the decimal points to the same number as your initial dataset. In our example, we have no decimal points, so we will reduce the mean number to a full number (see Figure A-11d).

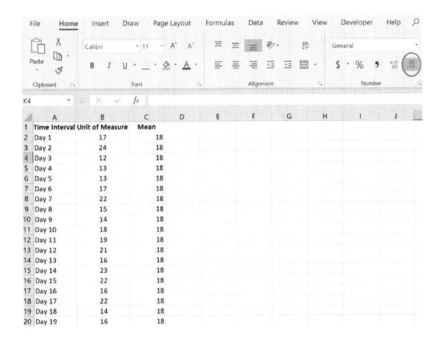

Figure A-11d: Formatting the Number of Decimals

STEP 5: Calculate the mR for the initial dataset, as shown in Figure A-11e. *Note*: leave a two-column space between the Mean and mR columns. We will use this space for adding the Upper and Lower Natural Process Limits.

	A	B	C	D	E	F
1	Time Interval	Unit of Measure	Mean			mR
2	Day 1	17	18			
3	Day 2	24	18			=ABS(B3-B2)
4	Day 3	12	18			
5	Day 4	13	18			
6	Day 5	13	18			
7	Day 6	17	18			
8	Day 7	22	18			
9	Day 8	15	18			
10	Day 9	14	18			
11	Day 10	18	18			
12	Day 11	19	18			
13	Day 12	21	18			
14	Day 13	16	18			
15	Day 14	23	18			
16	Day 15	22	18			
17	Day 16	16	18			
18	Day 17	22	18			
19	Day 18	14	18			
20	Day 19	16	18			

Figure A-11e: Calculating the Moving Range

STEP 6: Drag the calculated cell down to match the dataset selection, as shown in Figure A-11f.

	A	B	C	D	E	F
1	**Time Interval**	**Unit of Measure**	**Mean**			**mR**
2	Day 1	17	18			
3	Day 2	24	18			7
4	Day 3	12	18			12
5	Day 4	13	18			1
6	Day 5	13	18			0
7	Day 6	17	18			4
8	Day 7	22	18			5
9	Day 8	15	18			7
10	Day 9	14	18			1
11	Day 10	18	18			4
12	Day 11	19	18			1
13	Day 12	21	18			2
14	Day 13	16	18			5
15	Day 14	23	18			7
16	Day 15	22	18			1
17	Day 16	16	18			6
18	Day 17	22	18			6
19	Day 18	14	18			8
20	Day 19	16	18			2

Figure A-11f: Creating the mR Dataset

STEP 7: Calculate the XmR and create the dataset as shown in Figures A-11g and A-11h following the same steps as you did for calculating the mean value.

	A	B	C	D	E	F	G	H
1	Time Interval	Unit of Measure	Mean			mR	XmR	
2	Day 1	17	18				=AVERAGE($F$2:$F$20)	
3	Day 2	24	18			7	AVERAGE(**number1**, [nu	
4	Day 3	12	18			12		
5	Day 4	13	18			1		
6	Day 5	13	18			0		
7	Day 6	17	18			4		
8	Day 7	22	18			5		
9	Day 8	15	18			7		
10	Day 9	14	18			1		
11	Day 10	18	18			4		
12	Day 11	19	18			1		
13	Day 12	21	18			2		
14	Day 13	16	18			5		
15	Day 14	23	18			7		
16	Day 15	22	18			1		
17	Day 16	16	18			6		
18	Day 17	22	18			6		
19	Day 18	14	18			8		
20	Day 19	16	18			2		

Figure A-11g: Calculating the Mean mR Value

	A	B	C	D	E	F	G
1	**Time Interval**	**Unit of Measure**	**Mean**			**mR**	**XmR**
2	Day 1	17	18				4
3	Day 2	24	18			7	4
4	Day 3	12	18			12	4
5	Day 4	13	18			1	4
6	Day 5	13	18			0	4
7	Day 6	17	18			4	4
8	Day 7	22	18			5	4
9	Day 8	15	18			7	4
10	Day 9	14	18			1	4
11	Day 10	18	18			4	4
12	Day 11	19	18			1	4
13	Day 12	21	18			2	4
14	Day 13	16	18			5	4
15	Day 14	23	18			7	4
16	Day 15	22	18			1	4
17	Day 16	16	18			6	4
18	Day 17	22	18			6	4
19	Day 18	14	18			8	4
20	Day 19	16	18			2	4

Figure A-11h: Creating the mR Dataset

STEP 8: Calculate the UNPL and LNPL, as shown in Figures A-11i and A-11j.

	A	B	C	D	E	F	G
1	Time Interval	Unit of Measure	Mean	UNPL	LNPL	mR	XmR
2	Day 1	17	18	=C2+2.66*G2			4
3	Day 2	24	18			7	4
4	Day 3	12	18			12	4
5	Day 4	13	18			1	4
6	Day 5	13	18			0	4
7	Day 6	17	18			4	4
8	Day 7	22	18			5	4
9	Day 8	15	18			7	4
10	Day 9	14	18			1	4
11	Day 10	18	18			4	4
12	Day 11	19	18			1	4
13	Day 12	21	18			2	4
14	Day 13	16	18			5	4
15	Day 14	23	18			7	4
16	Day 15	22	18			1	4
17	Day 16	16	18			6	4
18	Day 17	22	18			6	4
19	Day 18	14	18			8	4
20	Day 19	16	18			2	4

Figure A-11i: Calculating the UNPL

	A	B	C	D	E	F	G
1	**Time Interval**	**Unit of Measure**	**Mean**	**UNPL**	**LNPL**	**mR**	**XmR**
2	Day 1	17	18	28.67444	=C2-2.66*G2		4
3	Day 2	24	18			7	4
4	Day 3	12	18			12	4
5	Day 4	13	18			1	4
6	Day 5	13	18			0	4
7	Day 6	17	18			4	4
8	Day 7	22	18			5	4
9	Day 8	15	18			7	4
10	Day 9	14	18			1	4
11	Day 10	18	18			4	4
12	Day 11	19	18			1	4
13	Day 12	21	18			2	4
14	Day 13	16	18			5	4
15	Day 14	23	18			7	4
16	Day 15	22	18			1	4
17	Day 16	16	18			6	4
18	Day 17	22	18			6	4
19	Day 18	14	18			8	4
20	Day 19	16	18			2	4

Figure A-11j: Calculating the LNPL

STEP 9: Create the UNPL and LNPL datasets, as shown in Figure a-11k.

	A	B	C	D	E	F	G
1	Time Interval	Unit of Measure	Mean	UNPL	LNPL	mR	XmR
2	Day 1	17	18	29	6		4
3	Day 2	24	18	29	6	7	4
4	Day 3	12	18	29	6	12	4
5	Day 4	13	18	29	6	1	4
6	Day 5	13	18	29	6	0	4
7	Day 6	17	18	29	6	4	4
8	Day 7	22	18	29	6	5	4
9	Day 8	15	18	29	6	7	4
10	Day 9	14	18	29	6	1	4
11	Day 10	18	18	29	6	4	4
12	Day 11	19	18	29	6	1	4
13	Day 12	21	18	29	6	2	4
14	Day 13	16	18	29	6	5	4
15	Day 14	23	18	29	6	7	4
16	Day 15	22	18	29	6	1	4
17	Day 16	16	18	29	6	6	4
18	Day 17	22	18	29	6	6	4
19	Day 18	14	18	29	6	8	4
20	Day 19	16	18	29	6	2	4

Figure A-11k: Finalizing our data analysis

STEP 10: Highlight the data we wish to showcase on the process behavior chart, as shown in Figure a-11l.

	A	B	C	D	E	F	G
1	Time Interval	Unit of Measure	Mean	UNPL	LNPL	mR	XmR
2	Day 1	17	18	29	6		4
3	Day 2	24	18	29	6	7	4
4	Day 3	12	18	29	6	12	4
5	Day 4	13	18	29	6	1	4
6	Day 5	13	18	29	6	0	4
7	Day 6	17	18	29	6	4	4
8	Day 7	22	18	29	6	5	4
9	Day 8	15	18	29	6	7	4
10	Day 9	14	18	29	6	1	4
11	Day 10	18	18	29	6	4	4
12	Day 11	19	18	29	6	1	4
13	Day 12	21	18	29	6	2	4
14	Day 13	16	18	29	6	5	4
15	Day 14	23	18	29	6	7	4
16	Day 15	22	18	29	6	1	4
17	Day 16	16	18	29	6	6	4
18	Day 17	22	18	29	6	6	4
19	Day 18	14	18	29	6	8	4
20	Day 19	16	18	29	6	2	4

Figure A-11l: Finalizing our data columns

STEP 11: Generate the process behavior chart following the green circles, as shown in Figure A-11m, and then adjust the colors of each line to get the sample graph in figure A-11n.

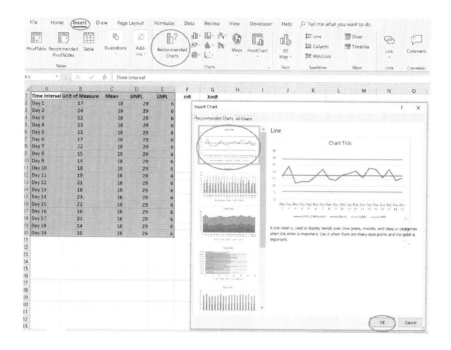

Figure A-11m: Generating a process behavior chart

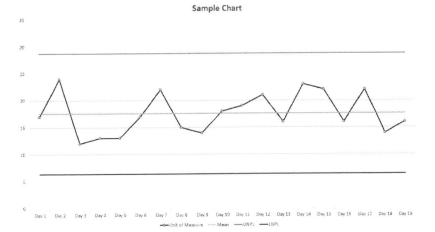

Figure A-11n: Process Behavior Chart sample

My Reflections Are

_____
_____
_____
_____
_____
_____
_____
_____
_____
_____
_____
_____
_____
_____
_____
_____
_____
_____
_____
_____
_____
_____
_____
_____
_____
_____
_____

My Reflections Are

My Reflections Are

_____

_____

_____

_____

_____

_____

_____

_____

_____

_____

_____

_____

_____

_____

_____

_____

_____

_____

_____

_____

_____

_____

My Reflections Are

Adjust the Process Behavior Chart

ONE IMPORTANT FACTOR TO remember is that: (1) your experimentation should cause signals on a predictable process that is far from the VOC, or (2) eliminate signals from an unpredictable process that you are trying to turn predictable. When you can correlate your improvement activity with the process behavior change, you can recalculate your process behavior mean and limits to depict those changes visually (See Figure A-12).

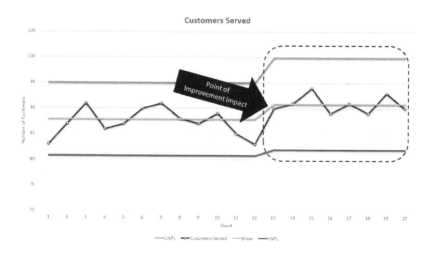

Figure A-12: Adjusted Process Behavior Chart

Coach's Reflection: Unless you have made improvements in your process, do not recalculate the mean or limit values. You have not improved the process behavior. You should focus on either shifting an unpredictable process to a predictable state or overhauling a predictable process to a new performance level. In that case, you will first create process signals that depict you are making an impact, and then focus on turning the process to a new predictable state. Consider this: If your process has a voice, what will it tell you?

Note: For further information on Process Behavior Charts, you can refer to Dr. Donald J. Wheeler's *Understanding Variation: The Key to Managing Chaos* – page 81.

My Reflections Are

My Reflections Are

My Reflections Are

Select a Dataset

WHEN YOU BEGIN GATHERING the data for analysis (process behavior chart development and interpretation), always ensure you are focusing on a specific process, even if it includes breaking down your process by product/service line or shift. For example, at one point in my career, I reviewed data from a hospital emergency department (ED). When the nurse manager pulled the data for the entire department, we came across a wide range in the natural process limits. When there is a significant variation between consecutive points, expect wide limits. In that case, we could be hiding signals under the noise blanket and misinterpret the process as predictable. When she separated the two shifts, however, we began to see a difference in the graphs by the mean value and natural process limits. Doing so will expose several process signals for the day-shift that were initially hidden in the broader limit range and initiate an obstacle-hunting mode, using the improvement KATA.

The same principle applies when you begin using the median versus the mean values of your process' performance, which will result in hiding some of the process signals within the natural process noise. Another example presented by Dr. Wheeler (2009, p. 65) is the quarterly sales figures for all regions. Putting all the data under one graph can showcase such wide limits that you would not be able to identify any process signals. Remember, each region is different. Therefore, you should never make the mistake of combining data from different operations because you will fall victim to hiding precious process signals under the wide process noise limits.

Do not exclude data from your dataset just because you feel it is not appropriate or caused by some random event. If randomness is part of how the process runs daily, then we need to see that, not pretend that it is not happening. The whole purpose of the process behavior chart is to open your eyes, remove the clouds built by your perception, and allow yourself to understand the context behind the data. Do not try to pick and choose the data points because you will only waste time doing so. If your process is screaming at you through the signals, please do not ignore them. Go and see the process, understand what is happening, collect the necessary data, and get to work.

Developing and interpreting the process behavior charts is only part of the scientific thinking lifestyle. Now, you need to begin improving the work. One good point to remember is that you do not need a plethora of data to start your journey. Identify your process, collect baseline data that do not include any change, and build your process behavior chart. Doing so will allow you to create an initial ecosystem that exposes you to the process signals as they happen or showcase how far the process behaves from the VOC. For example, if you have been running your distribution's pick-and-pack process, ED, or any production line without any changes made, collect ten data points, and begin building the charts. Separate product lines, shifts, and operators if you can. Narrow the data to get a clear picture of your process behavior chart. **There is nothing arbitrary or unintentional about scientific thinking.**

Coach's Reflection: If your data is infrequent (ex. Healthcare: number of CLABSIS per month) then you need to identify a better way to present that data. My experience has led me to use days-between-events when the data are infrequent, and it has allowed me to also expose patterns in the data. Do not let the lack of data stop you from innovating.

My Reflections Are

My Reflections Are

My Reflections Are

How to Utilize the Process Behavior Charts

EXPERIENCE HAS SHOWN THAT it is essential to observe the process steps and how employees operate, as well as understand the heartbeat of the process. The process behavior chart is the heart rate monitor of any process you wish to understand. Therefore, before you begin any improvement activity, I advise you to start by building the process behavior charts(s) associated with your area of interest. There are many paths you can choose to improve your process. The above is merely a suggestion that I have applied countless times in several processes and many different industries, and it works.

I am a big fan of always beginning an improvement journey by utilizing the Training Within Industry Job Methods process and pairing it with the Improvement/Coaching KATA. The merger allows us to grasp our current state and then innovate our process performance with the people involved in the process. For those not familiar with the concept of KATA, I advise you to review Mike Rother's The Toyota KATA practice guide. The same applies to Job Methods through the Training Within Industry Institute. Allow me to show you a few great examples from the healthcare industry regarding how you can do the same.

Through your strategic deployment process, you and your team have identified the Critical To Success (CTS) factors and the gaps you need to close. Pick one key performance indicator and expand on it. You will use an example from the healthcare industry and the indicator: improving product delivery accuracy from a healthcare distributor. You have the indicator identified, and you know how far you need to go this fiscal year. Instead of striving to achieve a specific number – ex. 99.5% accuracy – focus on trying to achieve a process behavior. An example of how you will write that goal: achieve a predictable process with a Lower Natural Process Limit of 99.5%. That statement tells you everything you need to know about the work ahead. You need to focus on achieving a much higher performance than 99.5% and develop a predictable process. That means no signals, especially from a direction that does not meet customer requirements.

Now that you have your challenge ready, you should begin understanding the VOP. Pull the data from the previous fiscal year by week. You will most likely come across large shifts from week-to-week and season-to-season. You will need to narrow down your focus. Who are the top 20% of your customers that account for 80% of your inaccuracies? Use a Pareto chart and identify your highest opportunity. Then, go back and pull the accuracy data by week for that customer. The variation should now be much less.

Think about how many different products you ship to that client. Repeat the above step regarding Pareto analysis, but this time focus on the chosen client's products. What are the top 20% of the products you ship that account for 80% of the inaccuracies you experience with your client? Pick the top offender. Now, pull the inaccuracy data for this product for the last fiscal year. How does the graph look now? It is probably much narrower on its variation compared to the one you started with. That is going to be your focus process. Follow the steps we discussed in previous chapters; pick the first ten data points to use as your mean and limits calculations, and build the process behavior chart. Do you see any signals? If you do not, then you have some investigative work to do. If not, then compare that product's delivery accuracy performance with what the customer requirements (VOC) are and how far off we are from those customer standards. If there are no signals and you are far from meeting the VOC, then you need to overhaul the process to begin fulfilling those requirements.

The next step is to utilize the Training Within Industry Job Methods process to identify the process details and characteristics that take place when your associates deal with that product. The process behavior chart has already given you an idea of what is happening, but you now need to see to understand. Take your team and go observe every step, every detail, and how employees think and operate on every shift that comes across this product. After collecting all necessary and available information, you can begin the process. First, develop the current working pattern step by step. What triggers the process, and when do we call this process completed? Is it when the product is on the truck, or when you file the paperwork? Did you observe anything during your investigation that you can track that shows how each process step performs? That can become a process behavior chart associated with your focus process. Remember, the process behavior chart for your overall delivery accuracy is what you will call the outcome metric. You will not work on that directly, rather, treat it as the outcome of all your work under the focus process. If you improve each focus process, then the overall outcome metric will head in the desired direction of your challenge. Now that you have grasped your current condition build the improvement KATA storyboard and follow Rother's four-step method to completion.

The above combination allows a coach to develop a learner regardless of her starting knowledge level effectively. We will primarily deal with front-line staff who do not work with data daily. The key-point on merging process behavior charts in your KATA journey is to develop the thinking and behaviors of the people. Avoid chasing after one point because that does not mean you have improved. Can you determine by one point on your graph if you have improved the process? Is that one point a sign of sustainment? A learner will eventually build the skillset to set a target condition going from chasing a data point to producing process signals. This new thinking behavior will help you develop a unique viewpoint for your employees if they work the process daily. It will also improve your coaching competency in identifying a learner's skill development gap. Your mission after reading and interacting with the material we have covered is to focus on improving a process behavior utilizing the charts that clearly depict when the change occurred. It is not easy, but I am confident that the information shared I have shared helped to expand your knowledge threshold. **There is nothing arbitrary or unintentional about scientific thinking.**

Coach's Reflection: The reason I highly suggest beginning your journey with the Job Methods process is that often as coaches we expect learners to see things as we do. To better fight that bias and help build a harmonious relationship between a coach and a learner, I suggest mentoring your team in understanding the process details. Asking the six questions associated with Job Methods process helps teams avoid a narrow mindset and question the context behind any process detail (Why is this necessary? What is its purpose? Where should it be done? When should it be done? Who is best qualified to do it? How is the best way to do it?).

Note: For further information on Process Behavior Charts, you can refer to Dr. Donald J. Wheeler's *Twenty Things You Need to Know* – page 19.

My Reflections Are

My Reflections Are

My Reflections Are

Dataset Examples

IN ONE OF MY coaching sessions, I came across a data availability obstacle. Specifically, the process-metric predicting how well the process performs was not available as a daily statistic. The quality-related event we were tracking was taking place infrequently, but when it did, it was devastating. As a team, we experimented and came across the opportunity to begin measuring the days-between-events as an option to populate our charts daily.

Do not hesitate to pinpoint changes in your charts and correlate them with your improvement activities. You should never try to explain every single point unless the point or set falls under each of the first three rules we discussed earlier. On the next page, in Figure A-14, not every activity led to an improvement in the process behavior. That is an excellent example to use to influence your team's perception of obstacles. Just because we perceive something as an obstacle, it does not mean it affects the process performance.

Referencing the process behavior chart in Figure A-14, you can show your team that their first activity in January led to an improvement in their process and anything that took place afterward helped create a predictable process. Therefore, after March, unless something extraordinary (signal) happens, we expect the process to operate within ~110 to ~142 minutes.

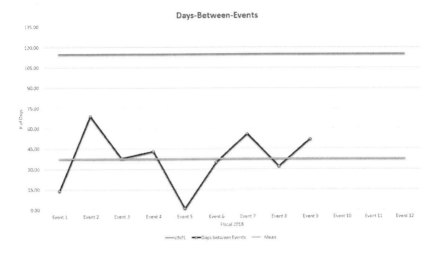

Figure A-13: Sample Process Behavior Chart

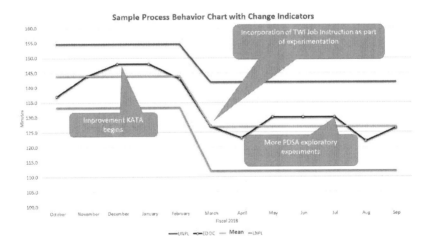

Figure A-14: Understanding Variation

My Reflections Are

My Reflections Are

My Reflections Are

The Moving Range Chart

As discussed in previous chapters, you must narrow your focus process and collect data for a specific activity, i.e., a product line on day shift, sales performance from a segment of our region, or financial performance from a specific value stream. Your process behavior chart should reveal the context you need to grasp your current condition. There are times, however, when you might need the help of the mR for greater insight. ***Be aware you should not let this section confuse you, but if it does, please skip this section and proceed to the next chapter.

If you are reading this paragraph, you are driven to learn more about mR analysis. I will keep it short and as informative as possible. If you have doubts that your process behavior chart does not show you any signals – a good indication is that your limits are too wide – then consider building and understanding the mR chart. You will build your mR the same way you built the process behavior chart. In this case, you will use the mR data as your main dataset, calculate the mean mR (XmR), and then only the upper limit using a different equation: Upper Range Limit (URL) = 3.269 x Mean(mR).

Use both behavior charts (Values & mR) to apply the four rules, as shown in Figure A-10, and begin your obstacle-hunting work. **Per the Process Behavior Interpretation Card in Figure A-10, only Rule #1 applies on the mR Chart.** The example in Figure A-15 represents patient quality-related events for an entire hospital. You will note, the original process behavior chart does not provide you with a signal other than the fact that the limits are too wide. This triggers you to follow the steps above and build the mR chart. The mR chart provides you with two signals recognized by the application or rule #1. Keep the Process Behavior Interpretation Card handy as your reference guide. Try to see to understand the context behind the data.

Note: For further information on Process Behavior Charts, you can refer to Dr. Donald J. Wheeler's *Twenty Things You Need to Know* – page 23.

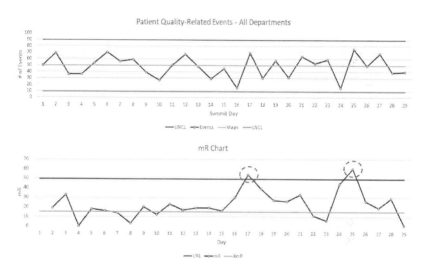

Figure A-15: mR Chart

My Reflections Are

My Reflections Are

My Reflections Are

Bibliography

Chamine, S. (2012). *Positive Intelligence.* Austin, TX: Greenleaf Book Group Press.

Graupp, P., & Wrona, R. J. (2016). *The TWI workbook.* New York, NY: CRC Press.

Heath, C., & Heath, D. (2008). *Made to stick.* New York, NY: Random House.

Heath, C., & Heath, D. (2010). *Switch.* New York, NY: Broadway Books.

Heath, C., & Heath, D. (2013). *Decisive.* New York, NY: Crown Publishing Group.

Heath, C., & Heath, D. (2017). *The power of moments.* New York, NY: Simon & Schuster.

Kotter, J., & Rathgeber, H. (2015). *Our iceberg is melting.* New York, NY: Penguin Random House LLC.

Kruger, J., & Dunning, D. (1999). Unskilled and unaware of it: How difficulties in recognizing one's own incompetence lead to inflated self-assessments. *Journal of Personality and Social Psychology 77(6)*, 1121-1134.

Lencioni, P. (2002). *The five dysfunctions of a team.* San Francisco, CA: Jossey-Bass.

Miller, J. G. (2004). *QBQ: The question behind the question.* Denver, CO: Penguin Group.

Rother, M. (2018). *The Toyota KATA practice guide.* New York, NY: McGraw Hill Education.

Welch, J., & Welch, S. (2005). *Winning*. New York, NY: Harper-Collins Publishers.

Wheeler, D. J. (2000). *Understanding variation: The key to managing chaos*. Knoxville, TN: SPC Press.

Wheeler, D. J. (2009). *Twenty things you need to know*. Knoxville, TN: SPC Press.

CASE STUDIES

Revenue Cycle

Background

The clinic partners with the hospital, under the same parent company, utilizing the hospital's operating rooms so the clinic doctors can operate on their patients. The hospital and clinic drop two different sets of charges to the insurance company: one for the patient's surgical fees from the clinic and one for the hospital's material usage. At its initial state, the third-party payer required the hospital and clinic to drop the charges differently which caused the hospital (initiator of the charges) to inaccurately place information as required by the insurance company for the clinic's portion of fees. The centralized charge filling by the hospital's administration did not capture the differences as are necessary for the clinic's charges, and no quality check was in place to ensure the process followed all the 3rd party payer requirements, always. That process caused several charges being returned and required refilling, which not only increased the days in accounts receivable (AR) but also lost revenue – as past 90 days, the third-party payers declined the charges. Leading the organization to begin writing off tens of thousands of dollars each year.

Performance Innovation

In May of 2018, the clinic's management team partnered with the Continuous Coaching Commitment's coach and initiated its performance improvement journey. Initially, the team identified the missed revenues as its priority challenge. They proceeded to grasp the current method by utilizing the TWI Job Method (JM). After several Go&See experiments, the team identified all the steps, characteristics, and data involved in the entire process.

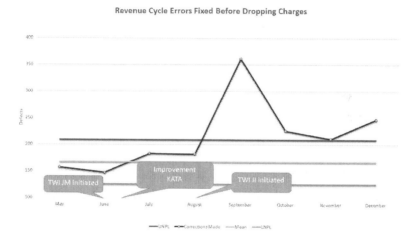

Figure A – CS1: Process Behavior Chart

Following the TWI JM process, the team defined a proposed state and began the identification of obstacles that prevented them from progressing to that level of performance. After several rapid PDSAs, the new process developed captured a mean of 167 defects on charges before sending them out to the third-party payers, resulting in $12K in bottom-line impact each month, as shown in Figures A – CS1 and B – CS1, below.

BOTTOM-LINE IMPACT

Figure B – CS1: Financial Impact

However, the team proceeded with re-applying JM on its now current method and found that due to variation in the review process and limited availability of resources, it required the utilization of TWI Job Instruction (JI) to institute standardization. In September of 2018, the team developed and successfully road-tested its process JIB. They developed and executed a training and validation plan. That increased the defects captured by 56%, which equated to an additional $7K in bottom-line profits each month.

Reflection

While the process could not be fixed at the hospital side – because the two entities belong to different organizations – it helped generate a higher bottom-line impact, even with the additional quality steps put in the process to ensure a higher rate of first-pass resolution rate (FPRR).

Patient Flow

Background

During a period of eighteen two-week target conditions, the healthcare outpatient care center (OCC) team achieved to increase their daily flow of patients by 15%, as well as continually improve on their patient satisfaction scores by two percentage points.

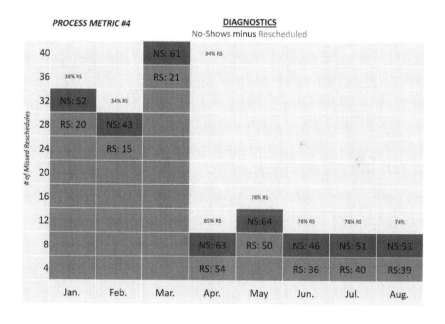

Figure A – CS2: Bar Chart

Typically, with the increased volume of patients, operations tend to break away from their standards, quality lacks, and patients experience a lower-level quality of care delivery. Utilizing Improvement and Coaching KATA, alongside TWI Job Methods, the OCC team succeeded by increasing their daily patient census by five and improving the quality of care delivery.

Performance Innovation

The team focused on identifying and understanding the obstacles preventing them from reducing the no-shows and therefore increase their daily patient volume.

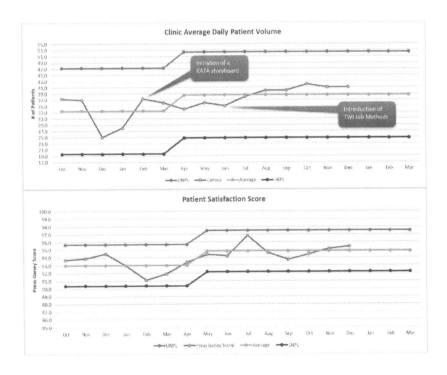

Figure B – CS2: Process Behavior Charts

The team's innovating thinking led them to improve the rescheduling effectiveness from 34% to above 78% within the first six target conditions – two each month – as shown in Figure A – CS2. The resulting 129% increase in rescheduling effectiveness allowed the team to create an immediate impact on their bottom line, both financially, as well as servicing their community, as shown in Figure B – CS2. The team continues to innovate its proactive communication process to improve the downstream appointment efficiency and reduce appointment cancelations further.

Reflection

The establishment of Improvement and Coaching KATA as the improvement foundation, alongside the TWI tools (Job Methods & Job Instruction), allows the generation of a continuous improvement routine. That routine leads to the consistent development of capability in both the process and the people involved.

About the Author

PANOS EFSTA FOCUSES ON organizational health. With 15 years experience developing management systems and people, he is an experienced performance innovation coach in the development of an organization's healthy management system through Strategic Deployment, Process Behavior Analysis, TWI Programs, and Improvement/Coaching Kata while developing competency (Dreyfus Scale), quickly. Taking everyone back to the basics, to achieve performance innovation. Panos' extensive experience in Healthcare, Services, and Manufacturing industries, alongside his education in business, healthcare, and finance, have allowed him to create a breakthrough approach with his client teams. One that promotes the evolution of the individuals' thinking to achieve operational excellence. Panos' coaching approach entails making each learner the storyboard of innovation, and once competency is developed, performance improvement begins. For more information, visit our website at www.piellc.us